Praise for Small Business Huge Success™ — Big Profits

"Having been in business for many years, I thought I had seen and read all the business tips going. Yet, I was amazed at the wealth of knowledge and variety of 'golden nuggets' Adèle has produced in her *Small Business Huge Success™ — Big Profits* book. Time and again, business books tend to focus on how to make profit whereas Adèle has correctly identified that reducing costs can be a shortcut to profit as well! Clear and concise, it features useful worked examples and some amazing personal stories that make you want to 'super boost' your own business. Buy two copies — the one you lend to a business friend won't come back!"

— **Shabbir Halai** CMIOSH, OSHCR — Director, Safety is the Key
www.safetyisthekey.co.uk

"Lots of small businesses will find issues here that are new to them and worth considering. I will happily recommend your book on the small business workshops I run."

— **Geof Franks** — Chartered Accountant
www.franks.co.nz

"An interesting insight into the world of business – a 'must read' for all new and existing business owners. The strategies highlighted at the end of each chapter are invaluable. An excellent and easy to follow guide that can be used to increase profitability. I will be recommending *Small Business Huge Success™ — Big Profits* to my clients."

— **Martin Ives** FCCA — Martin Ives & Co. Certified Accountants
www.martinives.co.uk

"I really enjoyed reading this book and it was great timing! I have recently taken the opportunity to research a business idea, source a supplier and start an online store. Your book is a thoughtful, well rounded reminder of the key areas that a small business needs to focus on. If your readers were to adopt just one chapter a month to focus on, at the end of the year there is no doubt that their business would be far more successful. Congratulations!"
— **Cara McNeilly** — Owner, Order and Progress
www.orderandprogress.com.au

"A superb book for those either buying a business, starting out in business or even established in business; this is brilliant for sharpening your entrepreneurial skills. Adèle McLay has covered every aspect of business, finance, systems and people development. This book must be the best buy of the year for an entrepreneur! Discover how to live in an entrepreneurial hotspot and get rewarded for it."
— **Sheena Walker** BA, CIPD — Master Coach, Mentor, Trainer and Teacher of Public Speaking
www.sheenawalker.com

"Having got to know Adèle McLay during the last year, I soon realised I had barely scratched the surface of her knowledge when reading *Small Business Huge Success™ — Big Profits*. The book is packed full of great advice in simple bite size chunks with live examples, and the *L⁴ Customer Profitability Quadrant* does it for me in much the same way as Robert Kyosaki and his Cash Flow Quadrant did many years ago. The principle of the *L⁴ Customer Profitability Quadrant* is easy to understand, and therefore, simple to adopt. Adèle is onto a winner here. Being in business is about learning from others and *Small Business Huge Success™ — Big Profits* removes many of the mysteries of working on your own success story."
— **Laurence Lowne** — Director, Combyne Group
www.combyne.wordpress.com

"Reading *Small Business Huge Success™ — Big Profits* is a must for any business owner who wants to achieve exponential business success. The straightforward strategies are like hidden treasures throughout and are incredibly powerful when applied. Adèle becomes a pocket mentor and paves the way for the business start up to achieve business success early on. The established small business will learn new strategies or be reminded of best practice actions to improve profit in no time at all. I'll definitely recommend *Small Business Huge Success™ — Big Profits* to my clients to help them achieve sustained financial success."
— **Cassie Footman** — Business Trust Coach
www.cassiefootman.com

"This book gave me the tools to really analyse my business, not only in terms of accounting and systems but also considering passion and emotion — factors which are often not discussed in these types of books. Adèle McLay explains how much real passion for what you do can tangibly increase productivity, and therefore revenue, and conversely how wasting energy on difficult clients and projects can decrease profitability. Now I understand why she uses the word 'Agitator' in her tagline; this book is like having a business coach come in, help you really look at your business and shake it thoroughly until it works more efficiently."
— **Kristi Milliken** — Director, Kingsland Osteopaths
www.kingslandosteopaths.co.nz

"I have had the pleasure of reading Adèle McLay's book and found myself wishing that this was something I'd read before I went into business for myself. I've learnt many of these lessons ... the hard way. It's a fantastic and easy-to-understand guide to many of the concepts that a business person should have a firm grasp on before he or she opens the doors. My own doors have been open for more than two years now and I've taken many of Adèle's ideas and implemented them, literally the day after reading the book."
— **Ricardo Da Corte** — Director, Minuteman Press Croydon
www.croydon.minutemanpress.co.uk

"Small Business Huge Success™ — Big Profits is a must read for all small business owners looking for huge success. Unlike the thousands of other business books that offer mountains of complex concepts, systems and approaches, Adèle's straight forward, no nonsense approach presents the key strategies in a highly effective, user-friendly and easily digestible manner."
— **Jackie Callaway** — Chartered Accountant, CFO, Director

"This book should be required reading for small business owners and anyone thinking about starting a business. It provides great advice on many subjects that are usually left out of business books on entrepreneurship."
— **Robert Rolih** — Entrepreneur and Author, Millionaire Money Making Machine
www.robertrolih.com

"This is a cleverly crafted, honest book to help everyone in business either start to earn decent money or to remind them why they are in business! I found the case studies were a true reflection of the book's intent and helped cement the reason to make sure your business is going to survive. It is fantastic that a straightforward read could provide the framework for the success of your business!"
— **Barbara Crestani** — Commercial Manager, E2 Digital
www.e2digital.co.nz

"I have loved reading *Small Business Huge Success™ — Big Profits*. It provides a wealth of knowledge for all business owners regardless of how experienced they are, helping them to be more profitable and successful. I especially enjoyed reading the entrepreneurial profiles. Their stories were illuminating and motivating. Just about everyone has challenges in owning a small business, and the entrepreneurs profiled are no different. Thank you Adèle. Your business experience and insights have been invaluable to me in my business, and I will be recommending your book to all other small business owners in my world."
— **Joanna Ellis** — NLP Trainer and Coach, Pure Confidence
www.pureconfidence.co.uk

BIG PROFITS

12 Strategies To Substantially Grow YOUR Business Profits

FOREWORD BY
RAYMOND AARON

NEW YORK TIMES BEST SELLING AUTHOR

By Adèle M. McLay

Akitu

AKITU PRESS

London, United Kingdom

First published in Great Britain in 2013 by Akitu Press Limited.
Akitu Press Limited, P O Box 56429, London SE3 9UF.

British Library Cataloguing in Publication Data.

A catalogue record for this book is available from the British Library.
Paperback Edition ISBN: 978-0-9926916-0-8
Digital Edition ISBN: 978-0-9926916-1-5

Photography by Jeff Oliver Photography: www.jeffoliver.co.uk
Book Design by Lucie Mauger: www.luciemauger.co.uk

To David, the love of my life; my greatest supporter and fan.
Thank you.

Contents

Acknowledgements

The vision for **Small Business Huge Success**™ is to provide relevant, accessible and digestible knowledge by way of books, learning programmes, and coaching to business owners around the world who want to learn more in order to achieve the business success and personal freedom they dream of.

I express my deepest appreciation to those who are supporting and contributing to bringing my vision for **Small Business Huge Success**™ to life.

First and foremost, thank you to my family, friends and staff who were extremely patient while I wrote **Big Profits**.

To David Hayde, my husband, who brainstormed the ideas for this book and critiqued me along the way, thank you. You are the best chartered accountant and management consultant I know, and I am very lucky that we are on the same team.

To Jackie Callaway, my friend, who also contributed ideas to the book, thank you. Your professional business experience and technical accounting abilities are second to none.

To Kathleen Tracy, my editor, your experience and knowledge has been invaluable. Thank you.

To Nicola Wilkinson, my loyal and long serving personal assistant, thank you for just getting on with it while I was working on this book, and for all your ongoing proof reading and editing.

To Lucie Mauger, my graphic designer and typesetter, thank you for your persistence in getting the layout for the book series looking fantastic!

To all my current and past clients — small and large businesses and charities that have allowed me to work with them over the last 20 plus years — thank you. It is through contributing my knowledge and experience in your organisations that I have grown professionally, and therefore, am able to write this book and the many more that will come within the **Small Business Huge Success**™ brand.

Finally, to our daughter, Gemma — my pride and joy. Thank you for letting Mummy write, even though you wanted to play or go shopping. I love you very much.

Foreword

I have committed my life to teaching powerful goal setting strategies and life management tools that dramatically change lives for the better. Whatever change someone is seeking, my purpose is to help.

In my experience, most people in business want to make more money and want more success, as they are the elements of the dream they have for their businesses and their lives. Oftentimes however, they don't set goals to achieve those dreams, and if they do, the goals are vague and not easily achieved. That's where I help. I help business owners to set fantastic and achievable goals.

So in reading **Small Business Huge Success™ — Big Profits,** I was delighted to read Adèle's no-nonsense, practical book, based on her experiences of consulting to and coaching small and large businesses towards greater financial success.

Adèle's book is packed full of easy to implement strategies that if applied to any business — big or small — will substantially increase profits, supporting business owners to achieve the financial and business success they have dreamed of and planned for.

This book is easily readable by all business owners. But, if you are unsure of how to implement any of the strategies, get help. Get your professional advisor to assist you to understand your business more, so you are in control of it and able to tweak it to achieve the goals you have set for your business success.

I just love the quote by Oliver Wendell Holmes — "The mind is like an elastic band; once stretched by a new idea, it never regains its original dimension." That is what this book will do for you and your business. It will stretch you with new ideas, and it will support you to achieve everything you have dreamed of in your business. So, get on with it. Read **Small Business Huge Success™ — Big Profits**, implement it, and enjoy your own Big Profits!

Raymond Aaron
Founder — Raymond Aaron Group™
Co-author, *Chicken Soup of the Soul* and New York Times
bestseller *Chicken Soup for the Parent's Soul*
Co-author, *Double Your Income Doing What You Love*
Author, *Branding Small Business for Dummies*

Introduction

> You don't have to see the whole staircase, just take the first step. **Martin Luther King Jr**

Hello from your adviser in business, or as I call myself, your personal 'Inspirator, Agitator, Motivator'™, supporting you to achieve everything you desire as a small business owner, including *BIG Profits*.

I've written this book to act as your mentor, adviser, and tutor all in one. I will also challenge you to make the business changes needed to achieve the financial success that you are seeking. By achieving huge financial success in your business, you will then be financially able to live the life you are seeking with your family and friends. Perhaps that means having a bigger home and car, more holidays — actually it means whatever you are seeking in your life to enable you to enjoy it to the fullest.

I live by the theme of **Dream It; Believe It; Achieve It** which resonates with me in all that I want to achieve, personally and professionally, even when the going gets a little tough. Perhaps it does with you too. Have a big dream for your business and life; believe that it is possible; then get on with achieving it, pushing through the setbacks. This book will help you create your own *Small Business Huge Success™*.

Easy Reading

When putting this book together, my goal was to make the information contained in it as accessible, relatable, and applicable as possible by using a direct, user-friendly format.

Bookshops are full of business books running into hundreds of pages. Who has time to read those? Certainly not me. But I strongly believe the key to growing and maintaining a successful business is to keep learning. We can never know enough.

However, learning doesn't have to be drudgery, slogging though endless pages of dense prose, so this book is packed full of facts and new knowledge, presented in a user-friendly, easily digestible style. The information is not dumbed-down; far from it. It's simply presented without the fluff, fillers, or waffle.

One Chapter, Every Day

The book's streamlined presentation of information makes it easy to read a chapter a day even if your schedule is jam-packed with other business and life tasks — or even if you are not a regular reader — and because I share these new concepts and ideas without unnecessary padding, you get the business knowledge delivered to your brain in record time.

Commit to reading just one chapter a day and in 10 days you will have absorbed powerful knowledge, which if implemented will bring dynamite potential to your business, resulting in *BIG Profits* and HUGE success.

Dip In When You Like

You don't have to read the book in any particular order so feel free to jump around. If certain chapters are more pertinent for you at the moment, dip in and read those first; generally speaking, it won't disrupt your understanding of the whole book.

Success Is Relative

By the end of this book, you will possess the tools you need to drive your business into the stratosphere of *BIG Profits* and HUGE success.

While success is relative and every entrepreneur has different goals, what all business owners need is a clear vision of what success means to *you* so you can pursue your goals with a focused determination you never thought possible.

Book Layout

I've attempted to make the book very easy on the eye, so that you can get through it quickly — and then head off to implement the strategies that resonate most with you and your business.

Most chapters include key points that are especially important to remember, so they are highlighted with a ! to ensure you don't miss them.

With respect, I will attempt to *agitate* you with my own comments at the end of each chapter; I simply want you, the small business owner, to be as financially successful as you would like to be, so I pose challenging questions or make points to stimulate thinking and action.

At the end of each chapter, I will also briefly summarise the chapter to help you take in the importance of the points made, in the hope that you will implement some or all of the key points of that chapter.

Target Audience

Many business books are written for entrepreneurs wanting to be the next Sir Richard Branson, Warren Buffett, or Bill Gates. There is nothing wrong with that, and I salute the endeavours of all entrepreneurs with those aspirations. If that is your intention, there is plenty in this book to help achieve that goal.

There are many small business owners who have a significant vision for their business and often have excellent technical skills, drive and energy to achieve their goal, but lack the broader business skills. This book is especially important for those businesses, as *Big Profits* will quickly steer you in the right direction towards achieving your vision.

Many small businesses aspire to simply make *BIG Profits* to complement a happy lifestyle. That delicate work-life balance can be so tricky to attain.

Luckily, regardless of the aspirations you have for your small business and your personal life, I've got a secret to share with you: it's not that difficult to achieve. The problem is many small business owners lose easy profits by spending too much time on the wrong things.

With a few tweaks and business tricks, I will show you how to set a course for *BIG Profits,* regardless of your aspirations for your business.

Inspiration, Agitation, Motivation™

My purpose with this book is to:

- Inspire you by providing you with new business knowledge.
- Agitate you into implementing the strategies from each chapter.
- Motivate you to achieve more in your business so you can enjoy the financial success you are seeking.

To that end, each chapter finishes with the success story of a small business owner who had a great idea, executed it well, and is now reaping the rewards of owning a hugely successful business. These inspiring entrepreneurs share the good, bad, and ugly experiences they encountered and the challenges they overcame on the way to achieving their goals. Some of the entrepreneurs have achieved massive success by anyone's standards, and others have achieved more modest success. Regardless, I believe their stories are inspiring and motivating.

So get ready to expand your business knowledge, gain a greater understanding of the key success drivers, and implement what you learn to ensure your small business is a HUGE success making *BIG Profits.*

"Sow a thought and you reap an act;
Sow an act and you reap a habit;
Sow a habit and you reap a character;
Sow a character and you reap a destiny."

Ralph Waldo Emerson

Chapter 1

Why Are You In Business?

> A dream business that doesn't make money is a living nightmare. **Habeeb Akande**

Over the past 20 years, I have supported and coached many businesses — large and small — in several different countries to improved financial performance. I will ask you the same question I ask all my clients:

Why are you in business? Think about it and then make a list of all the reasons.

1. _____

2. _____

3. _____

4. _____

5. _____

6. _____

Over the years I have heard a variety of responses:

- To be my own boss.

- To live my dream.

- To bring my product or service to market.

- To help others.

- To have a successful business.

- To make a difference and to make my customers happy.

- I am the ultimate entrepreneur and couldn't work for anyone else.

- To earn the money I am worth rather than receive a salary working for someone else.

- To control my life.

- To contribute to the lives of those who are less fortunate.

- To deliver social/community programmes.

While all of these answers are valid and in some cases even noble, they are not the reason you are in business. There is one reason and one reason only why you are in business: to make money — and hopefully, lots of it. I have to repeat this as it is so important:

Be in business to make money! And hopefully, lots of it!

There is no other reason to be in business.

Yes, establishing a financially successful business will enable you to achieve some or all of the above points, but they are not the principal reasons why you are in business. They are the results and benefits of being financially successful in business.

Over the years I have seen many small business owners not focus on the cashflow and profits — or lack thereof. The net result is that the business struggles with the owners living a hand to mouth existence, unable to achieve the dream they had set for themselves and their families.

Often, the owners work every possible hour just to make ends meet, sacrificing their own and their family's quality of life. In those situations, the business owner would be better getting a regular job, earning a steady salary instead of spinning their entrepreneurial wheels, working for what amounts to a couple of dollars an hour, and having no personal life.

Anyone who doesn't focus on profit and cash flow simply doesn't know enough about how to set themselves up to succeed. As author Michael Gerber notes in *The E-Myth*, owners need to spend more time working *on* their small business than working *in* it.

When a business is financially successful, it provides the owner with so many more opportunities, including:

- Growing the business and hiring staff, therefore contributing to the local economy.
- Contributing to and supporting the community through sponsorship and community involvement.
- Stepping away from the day to day business and allowing skilled managers to run it, while the owner focuses on the more strategic elements of the business.
- Providing time for continuing the owner's business education.
- Living the lifestyle the business owner dreamed about.

For example, look at the world renowned chef, Jamie Oliver. He has built a vast empire of restaurants; writes best selling cook books; creates fabulous TV cookery programmes; travels the world profiling good food; and enjoys a net worth of, at last count, approximately £100M. Jamie works hard, is hugely financially successful, and contributes to the community. In light of his success, he has also established the Jamie Oliver Foundation, which:

"aims to inspire people to reconnect with food. It's all about raising awareness and individual responsibility, resuscitating dying food culture around the world and, ultimately, keeping cooking skills alive."

Financial success in business enables a business owner to enjoy an expansive life beyond their business.

For all the challenges, self-employment offers many personal and professional opportunities as long as the owner controls the business rather than letting it control them. This saying sums up my sentiments exactly:

> **The worst day working for myself is still better than my best day working for someone else.**

In my opinion, there has never been a better time to start a small business. UK Trade Ambassador and businessman Lord Digby Jones believes small business "will lead the UK economy out of recession."

Regardless of the economy you operate your business in, small businesses will only lead economies out of recession if they themselves are financially successful. As famed investor Warren Buffett says: **'Rule No.1: never lose money; rule No. 2: never forget rule No.1.'**

I have a favourite saying:

> **Turnover is Vanity; Profit is Sanity; Cash flow is Reality.**

How many people do you know in business who gloat and say things like, "My turnover is in the millions," or "My business turnover is in the multimillions."

What a load of rubbish!

It may very well be that their turnover is in the millions, multimillions or even billions, but their business expenses could equally be in the millions, multimillions and billions — meaning, they could still be broke!

So turnover out of context means nothing. The key point is profit, the money left over after the operating expenses. It is also essential that businesses maximise their cash flow because you can't live on turnover and profit. You can only live on cash.

One of my businesses enjoyed a $2 million turnover with strong profits but the cash flow at times was a nightmare. While we had the best clients they were very slow to pay because of their internal systems. I know from firsthand experience that you can't pay staff and creditors when there is no cash in the bank, regardless of how profitable your business is.

I learned through the school of hard knocks how to effectively manage cash flow as well as ensuring I had a profitable business. I have since applied that knowledge to all my other businesses and to my consulting clients.

It drives me crazy seeing the amount of money and profit that businesses — big and small — lose out on through not properly managing their business affairs. I see it in every corner of business. The more you eliminate wasted opportunities, the more your business grows, and the more you reap the rewards of success.

Remember Your Dream

This book is not about setting goals. Rather, as you read though the book and learn new business concepts, I urge you to actively work on your business by implementing the strategies provided. Reading is one thing; implementation is another.

Before we move forward, take some time to reflect on the dream or vision you originally had for your business.

Dream It; Believe It; Achieve It!

> When it comes to money, you get what you truly intend to get. **T. Harv Eker**

What was your dream/vision you wanted to achieve when starting your business?

What will your lifestyle be like after achieving your business dream/vision? (Write about your home, personal income, holidays, family time, etc.)

If you have achieved your dream/vision already, how can you extend it to develop/grow your business? Go on, think really big. Create a new and massive dream/vision for your business.

When you achieve your bigger dream/vision, what will your lifestyle be like then?

How are you feeling when writing about your dream/vision for your business and lifestyle? Describe or draw the emotions you are experiencing.

> Feel the fear and do it anyway, and the death of that fear will be certain. **Susan Jeffers**

If the going gets a little tough as you implement the strategies presented in this book and you need a jolt of inspiration or motivation, take a moment to remember your vision, remind yourself of why you are in business, and know the strategies I'm sharing will have a direct and positive impact on your financial success.

Back to Basics

Before we get into exploring the 12 key *BIG Profits* strategies, I want to quickly review some fundamental business concepts.

Turnover

The term turnover is constantly interchanged with other words with similar meanings: gross sales, gross income, income, sales, revenue, and total income. All these words refer to the financial value your business generates by selling your products or services regardless of whether the customer has paid their bill. For business purposes, when you have supplied a product or service to a customer, you have made a sale.

Table 1a below demonstrates a simple example. Company ZZZ Limited sells two types of products and two types of services to its customers. The business made 500 sales in the year across the product range. What is their turnover or total sales?

	Unit Sales Price $	No. of Sales in Year	Total Sales per Product/Service $
Product 1	500	100	50,000
Product 2	1,000	100	100,000
Service 1	2,000	250	500,000
Service 2	5,000	50	250,000
Total Sales		500	900,000

Table 1a: ZZZ Limited - Total Sales

Gross Income

In this example, the total sales or gross income for ZZZ Limited is $900,000. That number tells us nothing about the success of the business. It simply says that the company supplied its products and services to its customers, and the value of the sales was $900,000.

As I mentioned earlier, many business people brag about their turnover, so in this instance, it might sound really impressive if the owner of ZZZ Limited said to you or me,   "My turnover was $900,000 last year."

A lot of people would be very impressed, but only if they didn't understand the real financial drivers of a business.

My response would be, "Lovely. Well done. What was your net profit after tax and how is your cash flow?"

That response would often cause the bragger to stop in their tracks because, as I said earlier, turnover tells us nothing about the financial success of a business.

Throughout this book, when necessary I will refer to turnover as gross income.

Gross Profit

Gross profit is a business's earnings after it has deducted the cost of producing its products and services for sale. Let's assume that ZZZ Limited's costs in producing its products and services are as set out in Table 1b.

	Unit Price to Produce $	No. of Sales in Year	Total Cost per Product/Service $
Product 1	200	100	20,000
Product 2	500	100	50,000
Service 1	1,000	250	250,000
Service 2	2,000	50	100,000
Total Cost of Products/Services		500	420,000

Table 1b : ZZZ Limited - Cost of Goods Sold

Using our example, the costs ZZZ Limited incurs to produce its products and services total $420,000. Those are the costs — generally referred to as cost of goods sold (COGS) — that are directly associated with production and not general office costs. Now that we know the production costs, we can work out the gross profit for ZZZ Limited as shown in Table 1c.

	$
Gross Income	900,000
Less Cost of Goods Sold	-420,000
Gross Profit	**480,000**

Table 1c: ZZZ Limited - Gross Profit

This shows that ZZZ Limited has $480,000 in profit remaining that is available to pay for the other expenses in running the business; specifically, the general office and staff expenses that were not incurred in producing the products and services it sold.

Net Profit

Next, to determine net profit, we need to identify the general expenses of ZZZ Limited. Net profit is generally referred to as net profit before tax and net profit after tax. In this example we are just looking at net profit before tax. In Table 1d I have listed the general business expenses of ZZZ Limited in abbreviated headings.

Expenses	$
Staff Costs	200,000
Office Rental	75,000
Advertising	50,000
Travel	3,500
Telecoms and IT	3,000
Entertainment	3,000
Office Stationery	2,000
Other	1,000
Total General Expenses	**337,500**

Table 1d: ZZZ Limited - General Expenses

The total of all the general expenses is $337,500, which is significant for the business. Let's see what happens when we deduct them from the Gross Profit.

	$
Gross Income	900,000
Less Costs of Goods Sold	-420,000
Gross Profit	480,000
Less Expenses	-337,500
Net Profit Before Tax	**142,500**

Table 1e: ZZZ Limited - Net Profit Before Tax

We now know $142,500 is the true net profit of ZZZ Limited before tax, which is a lot different from the $900,000 turnover/ gross income, don't you think?

Now you understand why I pay little attention when someone talks about their turnover as it generally has little relevance to the financial success of the business. Net profit is a far greater indicator of financial success.

However, net profit is a measure of profitability for only a period in time. It is usually determined at the end of a business's fiscal year as many small businesses do not do periodic accounts throughout the year.

Very often small business owners have no idea how their business is tracking from a financial point of view during the year because they don't receive monthly financial accounts. This is a mistake.

Getting an accountant "to do the books" at the end of the year is too late. You must manage your business's financial information on a monthly basis so you are fully in control of what is happening within your business and can respond accordingly. That is really not negotiable if you want to see *BIG Profits*.

Cash Flow

So often I hear business owners say, "I have a profitable business, but I never have any cash."

Lack of cash flow is a common problem. While net profit shows how financially successful a business has been over a certain period of time, it does not show a business owner how successful they have been in managing their business from a cash flow perspective.

If the cash that flows into the business consistently exceeds the cash flowing out of it, then the business will be sustainable. However, if the cash flowing out is consistently greater than the cash flowing in, then the business will eventually fail. Negative cash flow can occur in a business for a while as long as the business has cash reserves, but it cannot be sustained over a long period of time.

In my experience, small businesses are very vulnerable to cash flow crises, which is often a result of undercapitalisation at the start of the venture, leaving the business with little or no cash reserves.

It is critical to carefully monitor cash flow so in this book I am highlighting five strategies that can improve cash flow in your business.

Cash Flow Is Not Profit, and Profit Is Not Cash Flow

Business owners who do not have an accounting background often get confused by the distinction between profit and cash flow. Without wanting to get too technical — or boring — the fundamental principle of financial accounting is matching income and expenses during a discrete accounting period. For tax purposes, that period of time is a year, either calendar or fiscal. Monthly accounting periods are aggregated up to one year.

Cash flow, on the other hand, is impacted by cash received and cash paid out in the business at any time.

Return on Investment

Return on investment (ROI) is a simple formula that considers whether your business is making an adequate financial return on the money invested in it, or whether you would make a better return by placing the money in the bank.

I also like to calculate the ROI of a business owner's time in the business. Too often I see business owners working for too little financial return given the hours they work. I will *agitate* you about this again later in the book because I want all business owners to be thinking about valuing both their financial investment *and* their time investment.

The Basics are Understood

I have explained the basics of financial management, so it is now time to apply them to drive your business to greater financial performance and *BIG Profits*, so that you are achieving the dream you have for your business, and you and your family are also enjoying the lifestyle you desire. How does that sound?

Adèle McLay, The Agitator
Many business owners have strong skills in their specialist areas of business, but often lack a good understanding of the financial management elements of their business. I urge you to ensure you have a good grasp of basic financial management, using your accountant as necessary to enhance your understanding.

Dale Murray CBE

Co-Founder, Omega Logic; Angel Investor; Non-Executive Director; Government Business Adviser

Imagine starting up a business to launch technology based pre-pay mobile top-ups in the United Kingdom (previously a scratch card system was used), working incredibly hard with your fellow co-founders and staff to substantially grow the business in an exceptionally competitive industry, selling out and becoming CEO of the company that bought the business and driving mobile top-ups revenue to £450M, all in the space of approximately six years. Then being awarded British Angel Investor of the Year in 2011. Well, in a nutshell, that is Dale Murray's entrepreneurial story! But it doesn't end there. Dale is now a coach to start-up and early stage businesses. She is also a Non Executive Director (NED) of the British Government's Department for Business, Innovations and Skills, and UK Trade and Investment, along with being a NED of other businesses. Born in New Zealand and living in London, in 2013 Dale was awarded a CBE by HM the Queen for services to business.

There were many early challenges in establishing Omega Logic as a serious business in the mobile technology sector. Credibility was an initial hurdle as the company was very small and was competing with much larger and established technology software entities, all vying to win contracts with Vodafone, Orange and other multi-billion pound telecommunications network businesses. Professionalism, and a total customer service and delivery focus were key in being accepted and to winning major contracts.

The mobile top-up software developed by Omega Logic and other competitors was displacement technology. This required a change in consumer buying behaviour, which was not easy to achieve. Supported by the marketing efforts of the telecommunications networks and incentivising the re-sellers to sell top-ups rather than scratch cards, finally the new technology broke through consumer buying resistance, and Omega Logic grew. Dale and her co-founders had to 'dig deep' and totally believe that their technology would be accepted by consumers. "Resilience was often required", commented Dale, "as it was very difficult to push through the resistance in consumer buying patterns".

Another key element in Omega Logic's success was the quality of its technology. The company had a vision of being the best software provider for top-ups on the high street, leveraging the till technology that retailers already had.

Strong financial management was also key to the success of Omega Logic. Dale has a chartered accounting background, and ensured robust financial control systems were in place to manage the volume of money that flowed between the retailers, networks and Omega Logic.

Dale's advice to budding entrepreneurs is: 1) Clearly understand and articulate what it is you are doing – what is the business? What problem are you solving and how are you going to make money? If over time there is a lack of clarity around the business strategy, quickly sort it out to enable the business to move on. 2) Carefully manage team dynamics. When things go wrong with people (founders and staff), face them head on, and deal with them immediately. 3) Network widely from time to time, but get on with the work. Dale notes that too many budding entrepreneurs are focused on networking rather than building their business.

Over the next few years Dale wants to continue acting as an advocate for entrepreneurs in all the various capacities she currently enjoys. Dale has a particular interest in female entrepreneurs as she believes they see things differently. As well, Dale will continue investing in ventures that are of interest to her.

Adèle's Note: Dale has a wonderful entrepreneurial success story, founded on being in the right place at the right time; being in a sector she knew and liked; with her co-founders, working exceptionally hard to break into and succeed in an established market; being totally focused on customer service and software excellence; and having a total passion for and belief in what Omega Logic stood for, especially when times were tough. As well, the co-founders had an exit strategy that they executed at the right time. Since then, Dale has continued her entrepreneurial endeavours, while supporting others towards their success. Dale now has three young children, and while she gets huge pleasure out of business, she is very family focused, and able to balance the demands and joys of both. It was an absolute pleasure to interview Dale, and to hear her story which will be an inspiration to many entrepreneurs across the world.

To connect with Dale Murray CBE:
W: www.dalemurray.net
Tw: @dalejmurray

Chapter 2

Cash Flow: The Life Blood Of Business

> Cash flow is a critical business driver in any business and needs to be monitored carefully.
>
> **Adèle McLay**

Cash flow is the sum of all the cash received into your business, less all the cash payments being made from your business. Positive cash flow is when there is more cash coming into the business than being paid out of it. Negative cash flow is when there is more cash being paid out of the business than is being received by the business.

As I discussed in Chapter One, businesses mostly focus on gross income and net profit — before or after tax. While both are important in business, cash flow is the life blood of all businesses, and without it they eventually die.

Think about blood in relation to your body. If you lose all your blood, you will die. It is the same in business: have no cash and the business will eventually fail. While a business can sustain a negative cash flow for a while if it has ample cash reserves, most small businesses do not.

Yet, sadly, very few business owners spend much time thinking about cash flow or understand how critical a business driver it is.

The key transactions in business that affect cash flow are:

- Sales (cash and credit).
- Purchases (inventory and business expenses).
- Business loans (new and repayments).
- Business assets (buying and selling them).
- Investments (new and repayments).

Profitable businesses are not immune from cash flow issues. Remember that profit is determined by matching income with expenses, whereas cash flow is determined by cash received and paid out. To demonstrate my point, let's look at how a profitable business can be seriously affected by inadequate cash flow management.

Let's assume BBB Limited has just been established, taking a new product to market where sales will be $5,000 the first month and then will double each month thereafter. Customers are given the standard 30-day payment terms. However, BBB Limited has to buy their inventory for cash, as they are a new company with no credit history with the supplier. The inventory will cost 40 percent of retail price, or has a gross margin of 60 percent. General business expenses will be 20 percent of turnover each month and are paid by month end at latest.

Look at the profitability and cash flow effects on this business after six months in business as shown in Tables 2a and 2b.

	Month 1 $	Month 2 $	Month 3 $	Month 4 $	Month 5 $	Month 6 $	Total $
Gross Income	5,000	10,000	20,000	40,000	80,000	160,000	315,000
Less Cost of Goods Sold	-2,000	-5,000	-10,000	-16,000	-32,000	-64,000	-129,000
Gross Profit	3,000	5,000	10,000	24,000	48,000	96,000	186,000
Less Expenses	-1,000	-2,000	-4,000	-8,000	-16,000	-32,000	-63,000
Net Profit Before Tax	2,000	3,000	6,000	16,000	32,000	64,000	123,000

Table 2a: BBB Limited - Profit and Loss Statement for Six Months

	Month 1 $	Month 2 $	Month 3 $	Month 4 $	Month 5 $	Month 6 $	Total $
Cash In	0	5,000	10,000	20,000	40,000	80,000	155,000
Less Cash Out	-3,000	-7,000	-14,000	-24,000	-48,000	-96,000	-192,000
Net Cash Flow	-3,000	-2,000	-4,000	-4,000	-8,000	-16,000	-37,000

Table 2b: BBB Limited - Cash Flow Statement for Six Months

What do you notice? The profitability of BBB Limited is strong at \$123,000 profit for six months. However, in the same period it also has a negative cash flow of \$37,000, which means there is more cash going out of the business each month than is being received. This is a scary situation for the owners of BBB Limited, especially if the business is relying on a bank overdraft to fund the negative cash position.

It is likely that the accountant for BBB Limited will say, "Very well done. You have a successful business," while the bank manager will say, "You can't extend your overdraft any further," or worse, "We are cancelling your overdraft."

The business owner will be totally confused and stressed. After all, haven't they got a successful business?

While this is an imaginary example, it demonstrates the point that if cash flow is not managed carefully, a successful business can be crippled and will die if it does not have cash reserves in its bank account.

The cash flow issues in this example could easily be magnified if any or all of the following occurred:

- Debtors take longer than 30 days to pay.
- Debtors don't pay at all.
- Inventory prices increase without a corresponding increase in sales price.
- Bank interest rates increase dramatically.
- Sales price is reduced due to competition.
- General business expenses increase out of proportion to the growth in the gross income.

As you can see, managing cash flow in a business can be tricky and is critical.

In this chapter you will find five strategies that, if implemented, will have an immediate impact on your business cash flow and, at times, profitability.

Collecting Payments for Sales

Most business owners discover the joys of debt collecting at some point. In accounting terms, we have a little formula called the *accounts receivable ratio* — very original, right? — that tells us how successful we are at collecting money from our customers. Accounts receivable are the monies owed by customers to whom we have extended credit terms for payment. If a business sold all its products and services for cash, then it would not have accounts receivable. Very few businesses deal entirely in cash so the vast majority have accounts receivables.

The accounts receivable ratio is calculated as follows:

$$\textbf{Accounts Receivable Ratio} \ = \ \frac{\textbf{Gross Income for the Year}}{\textbf{Total Accounts Receivable Outstanding}}$$

For example, if the gross income in your business was $500,000 for the last year and you currently have $75,000 of accounts receivable owed to you, then your accounts receivable ratio would be: 500,000/75,000 = 6.67

To determine how long on average it takes for your customers to pay their accounts, we then divide 365 (days in the year) by that number 365/6.67 = 55 days.

Now this is interesting, because if your customer payment terms are less than 55 days, which they likely will be, then your customers are being very slow to make payments to your business, and your business cash flow is being seriously affected as a result.

Think about it. If your payment terms are 30 days or less and you are getting paid on average at 55 days, something needs to change.

Let's look at all the ways in which you can improve the cash flow into your business by better managing your accounts receivable systems and processes.

Better Invoice Details

When working with my coaching clients, the first thing I look at is a client's invoice template. I am constantly staggered by the number of invoices I see sent by my clients to their customers that do not include the *payment due date* or *payment instructions*, including bank account information for online payments.

I recently asked one of my staff to review all the invoices received by all my companies over the last year to gauge how many invoices we received without this basic information. We found that 70-80 percent of the invoices did not contain one or both of these basic instructions. This is obviously a lost opportunity for small businesses. When this basic information is not present on invoices sent to my businesses, we immediately put them into the 30 days payment category and they will not be paid earlier. Again, this is not great for a small business owner, where cash flow may be an issue.

Recently a painter undertook some redecoration work for one of my properties, and duly emailed the invoice without a *payment due date* or *payment instructions* attached. We immediately coded the payment as 30 days, and I then went on holiday. While away, the contractor left a telephone message saying that he had cash flow issues, and would I pay his invoice, and that he was 'sorry to chase me for payment'. I was away and couldn't pay the invoice, so he had to wait until my return from holiday to be paid, which was at the end of the month – 30 days after he submitted the original account. Now if he had asked for seven days or any other payment date, I would have arranged to have it paid while I was away by setting up a forward date payment in my online banking system, and therefore, I could have assisted him with his cash flow challenges.

I wonder how many small businesses around the world operate like that?

I think the key issues here are lack of knowledge on what to include on an invoice, and/or fear. If a small business owner is making up their own invoices, often they don't think about what should be included on an invoice to a customer, or if they do, they are fearful of putting a payment due date on it, perhaps fearing the customer will complain about their terms of business.

After a product is sold or a service delivered and the invoice is produced, it is your duty as a business owner to let your customer know exactly when you expect the invoice to be paid and how they can pay it (via cheque, credit card, online portal, PayPal, etc.). If you do not, then they will pay whenever they get around to it. That decision has an immediate impact on your business's cash flow.

Similarly, omitting payment options and instructions from invoices creates missed opportunities to get paid by online banking or some other form of digital service. In my businesses, it's often not until we go to pay our bills that we realise payment options and instructions are missing on the invoice. So my staff have to telephone the creditor and get the information sent by email as we do not accept payment instructions verbally or by text. That's a waste of everyone's time, energy, and resources. It is also bad cash flow management for the business awaiting payment from us.

Given that most consumers live in the information age, I would go so far as to suggest that the business owner writes on the invoice that they prefer payments to be made via online banking rather than by cash or cheques. That way, when the payment is made the cash arrives in the business owner's bank account as cleared funds immediately. Whereas with cheques, the business owner will have to visit the bank to deposit the cheque and then wait until the bank clears it before they have access to the funds.

Not every customer will pay online but eventually they will, as cheques will eventually phase out, so start training your customers now on how to do business in the modern world.

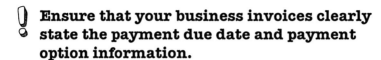

Ensure that your business invoices clearly state the payment due date and payment option information.

Payment Terms

Again, using my own experience, I find many small businesses say their payment terms are 30 days after receipt of invoice. I often wonder why they extend so much credit, as generally payment terms will not be a negotiating factor for a small business with their customers. If you are sending an invoice after you have done the work, why not make your payment terms seven days?

In my businesses, we pay our accounts according to when the supplier says they are due and not a day earlier. If the supplier says it's 30-day payment terms that is when we will pay it. If they say it is a seven day payment term, then that is when we pay it.

Also, many people do not pay their accounts on time regardless of the length of the payment terms. Therefore, the shorter the payment terms you give, the quicker you can start following up with a customer who has not paid by the due date. Which would you prefer — to get paid seven or so days after you have sent an invoice or sometime after 30 days? I know what I would prefer.

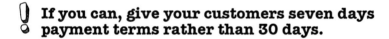

If you can, give your customers seven days payment terms rather than 30 days.

Sending Invoices

Many small businesses bill their customers at the end of the week or at the end of the month. I am not a fan of this approach at all and in my coaching business I actively encourage my clients to send invoices by email or post on the day the product or service was delivered if they are not able to give the customer the invoice on the spot.

Suppose my refrigerator broke down and I needed a specialist to come out and fix it. Let's say they arrived on the first day of the month and fixed my refrigerator. But the business was so busy they didn't bill me until a week later; or worse, they waited until the end of the month, and I had 30 days payment terms. If this was a real situation, the repair company would not get paid for almost two months after the work was completed. Great for me; not so great for the business.

> **Reduce the payment terms on your invoices and send them out the same day. If possible, hand the invoice to your customer before you leave them.**

Payment on the Day

Think about the payment terms of a retail or online shop. As customers, we can shop to our heart's content, but we don't get to take the goods until we pay for them. This is great for the retailer because they get their money immediately at the time of purchase.

So why are small businesses not adopting the same payment model? Why do they extend credit terms to their customers?

The simple answer: because that's the way it's always been done. They have never thought about operating their businesses in a different way to protect their cash flow.

I strongly believe there is a considerable opportunity for many small businesses to change the way in which they do business. Technology is fantastic for enabling businesses to work smarter. To receive same-day payment for their work a small business just needs to invest in credit and debit card processing systems and equipment.

Let's go back to my broken refrigerator experience. In reality, the technician who comes to fix our appliances does not invoice us later. He takes payment on the spot either by cash, debit or credit card. When I call to make an appointment the office manager gives me an estimate of what the appointment will cost.

The technician often has to make two visits: the first to determine the problem and, if necessary, a second to replace any parts he needed to order.

Before leaving, the technician prepares an invoice for the work done on that visit and I pay by credit or debit card. He also quotes me the exact cost of any parts he ordered and what the labour cost will be for the second visit. I know where I stand in terms of further costs, and he has been paid for his work on that visit.

This business is very clever. They realised that if they did not collect payment from their customers on the day, the chances were high that they would have a major cash flow issue as they have to order and hold items of inventory for customers. This repair business has no residential accounts receivable outstanding at all and I love it.

So many businesses could do the same, especially trade businesses such as electricians, plumbers, and handymen to name a few, when they are working with residential customers rather than corporate or business clients.

 How can you re-organise your business so you always receive same-day payment with residential customers?

Credit and Debit Card Facilities

Cheques are fast becoming relics of a bygone era and most people do not carry large volumes of cash with them when shopping. If your small business has been operating for a minimum of two years and has a good credit history, most banks will offer merchant facilities - the ability to accept debit and credit payments. The fantastic thing is that if you take up this opportunity, seldom will you have accounts receivables. It is all a matter of re-educating your customers on how you conduct your business.

Credit and debit card facilities are worthwhile in all businesses even if you do not want to take payment immediately. By giving your customers the option of paying by debit or credit card rather than sending a cheque, when you are paid you get automatic access to the money because in most cases banks transfer funds on the same day. Plus, not all customers will remit payment online so debit and credit card facilities are the next best thing in terms of getting access to your payment immediately.

Credit and debit card merchant facilities are not free. The banks charge a fee to process each transaction. Depending on the bank you approach, the level of the fee may be negotiable, but it will usually be dependent on the volume of business undertaken via the merchant facilities.

For small businesses where they have a large volume of small value transactions with their customers, merchant facilities provide a quick and easy method to get paid without having to create official invoices, undertake accounting administration, and devote resources to debt collection when not paid on due date.

> **Rethink the way in which your small business operates. Consider taking on merchant facilities to receive debit and credit card payments.**

Following-up on Invoices

I accept that not all businesses will be able to change their business to take payment on delivery or after the work is done. If you are a business that will always need to send your customers an invoice, then there are ways to speed up the payment process to ensure the money is paid into your bank account as soon as possible.

In my New Zealand consulting business, we worked with all the large national corporations and while they were excellent clients, getting payment could be a considerable challenge at times due to their internal processes, which often left my business with a negative cash flow at critical times, such as the end of the month when all the staff salaries, rental accommodation, and monthly expenses were due. It was not an easy time. It took a while to address the situation but the following process usually worked.

As soon as the invoice was sent, my office manager's job was to call the line manager to check that they had received the invoice and to ask if they had signed it off for payment.

If they had not, then the telephone call was a gentle and very polite reminder to the manager. If they had, then my office manager would simply thank them politely.

Once she knew the payment had been approved by the line manager, my office manager would then telephone the accounts payable department to see if the bill had been entered into the client's payment system, and if so when it would be paid. If not, she would back track to find out what the problem was and work to resolve any issues so that the invoice was in the system for payment.

The key to the success of this system we developed was my office manager's interaction with our clients. We had repeat customers so over time the office manager built a relationship with the accounts payable department staff and the line managers, and it was all very amiable. Also, once our clients knew that we had a system in place to ensure our accounts were processed in an orderly and timely fashion, the line managers usually responded by signing off our accounts immediately. In some cases, the office manager didn't need to call them as she knew they would sign off the invoices the day they arrived at their desk.

By implementing this system, we always knew when our accounts would be paid by our clients, so I could then manage cash flow more easily.

Yes, it took a lot of time, but that was part of my office manager's job and she enjoyed it. It was much more uncomfortable to ring creditors to say we couldn't pay at month's end due to cash flow than it was to implement an accounts collection system that ensured our clients paid on time.

I can hear many business owners reading this and saying, "You had an office manager, but I work by myself. I don't have time to do that."

I understand that perspective. But if you do not have someone in your business or personal life who can support you with the very important task of collecting your money, then consider employing the services of a virtual personal assistant. A virtual personal assistant is someone who works for your business on a part-time/occasional basis, and often works away from your business. Virtual personal assistants, if properly trained by you, are worth their weight in gold and can help a small business owner in so many ways.

Plus, they will not break your bank. Most virtual PAs are very cost effective. Once a small business owner builds a relationship with a highly skilled virtual PA, they will realise there is so much more these people can do for them to support the success of their business, freeing the owner up to do what they do best: managing the growth and success of their business.

 How can you re-organise your business to ensure all invoices sent to customers are followed up?

Early Payment Discounts

If your business or industry can't collect payment on the day the product or service is delivered, consider introducing an early payment discount. This is especially important if your usual terms of payment are 30 days and you will not or cannot change them. Incentivising your customers to pay early with a percentage discount is commonplace in many industries; utilities companies are well known for this.

Typically, businesses offer a discount of 5-10 percent to encourage early payment of invoices. While early payment discounts reduce the amount of cash received by a business, in most situations that is preferable to the small business than having large volumes of accounts receivable outstanding, which has a considerable impact on cash flow.

Can your small business offer early payment discounts to your customers to encourage early payment of outstanding invoices?

Factoring Your Invoices

Factoring invoices is not for all businesses, but for those that sell their products and services to other businesses (meaning they are operating in the business to business (B2B) market) and have an ongoing invoice collection issue, factoring can be the answer to cash flow challenges.

What is factoring? It is a simple solution to cash flow. A factoring company purchases the invoices you have sent to your customers and within one or two days will pay you between 80 to 90 percent of the value of the invoices. The factoring company will then collect the payment from your customer directly. Once paid, the factoring company will pay you the balance of the account less their fees, which are typically between 1 and 5 percent of the invoice. The fees charged depend on a number of factors including the credit period your business has given to your customer and the credit worthiness of your customer. The factoring company makes an assessment on likelihood of collection of the account and the value of the credit invoices you submit.

If your customer has an excellent credit record, is financially stable, and your business has extended credit to that customer for a maximum of 30-60 days, then your business can get the best rates for your credit invoices. However, if your business has given your customer extended credit to around 90 days and the customer's credit record is marginal or poor, then the fees you will pay to factor the account will be higher.

The advantages of factoring can be significant because your business receives cash even though you have extended credit to your customer. The cash you receive enables your business to properly function, paying staff and bills and purchasing inventory and equipment.

There are also some drawbacks to using factoring as a tool, which should be understood and investigated before implementing this method of improving cash flow.

If the credit period you extend to your customer is too high, or if the factoring company determines your customer's credit rating is marginal or poor, then the fees it will charge you can be at the high end of the spectrum. There may be cheaper ways to collect the debt in this instance.

Also, if there are problems with collecting the payment, there is a chance the staff at the factoring company responsible for collecting the payment could upset your customers. This possibility must be weighed against the relationship your business has with your customer.

Finally, if the profit margins in your business are low, then the added cost of factoring invoices may prove to be too expensive.

> **If you are operating in the business to business market, consider whether factoring your invoices to a reputable factoring company offers enough benefits as a tool to enhance your business's cash flow.**

Invoices vs Statements

An invoice is sent after every piece of work is undertaken. A statement is sent to a customer at the end of the month detailing all the invoices issued to the customer during the month, plus it records any outstanding balances to be paid from previous months.

Many businesses do not send statements to their customers. I believe this is a lost opportunity. If you do not take up my suggestion of telephoning your customers to check on payment progress, issuing a statement lets the customer see what invoices they should have received and should have paid. Often invoices get misplaced or buried under other mail. A month end statement detailing all invoices sent will hopefully enable your customer to reconcile their outstanding accounts with your business and get them paid on time.

If your business is using professional accounting software to process your accounting affairs, most are set up to print out monthly statements with a few keystrokes.

> **Set up your business accounting system to ensure it enables you to easily print out and send statements to all your active customers at the end of every month.**

Paying your Suppliers

So far, we have talked about managing the cash flow in your business by controlling your accounts receivable processes. However, your business also has to pay its own accounts, so you are a creditor to other businesses.

Purchasing and Payment Terms

Perhaps your business consistently buys stock and other items from the same supplier. If so, then as a business owner you should be talking to the account manager you have with the supplier and asking for better terms when buying your goods. This could include negotiating better buying prices for the goods you are buying, given you are a loyal customer. As well, you can negotiate your own payment terms, perhaps asking for 30 days payment, or longer if you can negotiate it. If the supplier is a big company, you may well have success in reducing your pricing and agreeing extended payment terms, especially if the supplier values your business as a loyal and good customer.

Shopping Around for Discounts

If your business is not a big buyer of supplies from any one supplier, then by using the internet you may be able to buy the goods and services you need at cheaper prices if you shop around. The challenge with this method is that you will have to pay at the time you purchase. However, the reduced price of the goods may well counterbalance the requirement to pay at the time of purchase.

These days in many countries a business can order online and the goods will be delivered a day to two later. That type of delivery service is excellent in helping a small business reduce the amount of inventory it needs to hold for their business. So, while having to pay for the goods at the time of purchase, there may be other benefits to purchasing via the internet, as holding too much inventory within a business is also a considerable drain on cash flow.

Managing Your Inventory

Like accounts receivable and payable, inventory plays a key role in managing a business's cash flow. For many businesses, inventory is the single biggest asset they will have on their balance sheet. Again we have a little accounting formula that tells us how well we are *turning over*, or selling, our inventory every year:

$$\textbf{Inventory Turn} = \frac{\textbf{Annual Cost of Goods Sold}}{\textbf{Average Inventory}}$$

$$\textbf{Average Inventory} = \frac{\textbf{Beginning Inventory} + \textbf{Ending Inventory}}{2}$$

If the cost of goods sold is \$300,000 and the average value of the inventory you are holding is \$50,000, then your *inventory turn* is \$300,000/\$50,000 = 6.

This means that you are selling or turning your inventory six times in the year.

The higher your *inventory turn*, the better your cash flow, as you have less inventory sitting around waiting to be sold. Conversely, the lower your inventory turn the worse it is on your cash flow, as it means you have a lot of money tied up in inventory in your warehouse that is waiting to be sold.

A low *inventory turn* may indicate that your business is holding inventory that is obsolete. If your business is holding large inventories in certain product lines, those products may have some inherent problems that could lead to obsolescence. It could also mean that the marketing of the product line is not successful and needs to be addressed with the marketing department if you have one.

Similarly, a very high *inventory turn* can indicate that your business is not effectively managing its inventory levels and may well lead to loss of business if your business receives a big order that cannot be fulfilled in a reasonable time due to inventory not being available. So there is a fine balance between holding too much and too little inventory.

Inventory holding is an especially important consideration if your business is currently expanding. Continuing with the earlier example, let's assume that the business doubled its sales to $1,000,000 in the following year. What impact would that increase have on the need to hold inventory?

Inventory holding is calculated as:

$$\textbf{Inventory Holding} \;=\; \frac{\textbf{Annual Cost of Goods Sold}}{\textbf{Inventory Turn}}$$

If the gross profit margin is 50 percent, then the cost of sales on $1,000,000 would be $500,000. With an inventory turn of six, the business would need to ensure it was holding inventory of $83,333 to ensure it could deliver on the sales ($500,000/6 = $83,333).

Given the inventory holding the previous year was $50,000, the business is going to have to find an extra $33,333 in cash flow to buy the inventory to service its increased sales. If the cash or credit cannot be found to cover the increased need to hold inventory, then the growth of the business will be negatively affected.

Many businesses carry a range of inventory items in their business, each of which *turns* at different rates. To truly manage the cash you have tied up in inventory, you need to analyse the individual inventory turns for each product and then determine the optimal holdings of inventory item according to its inventory turn.

Purchasing Assets vs Hire Purchase vs Leasing

When a business has cash in the bank, it is very tempting to use the cash to make major asset purchases like equipment and motor vehicles. This is a BIG mistake. Never use your surplus cash to make lump sum payments on assets. There is a better way.

A business needs to have cash reserves for the times when business is difficult, so put the cash in a savings account that you can access when necessary and leave it there as a business buffer for times when you really need to use it.

When your business needs to purchase equipment and motor vehicles or other major assets, it is far more preferable for your business to consider using tools like leasing or hire purchase to buy the asset.

How Leasing Works

When you want to purchase a piece of equipment or motor vehicle, a finance company will buy it for you and rent it to your business. That means rather than paying the full purchase price up front, your business will pay to rent it each month in accordance with the contract period as agreed to between the finance company and your business. At the end of the contract period, you can buy the asset from the finance company at a reduced price, called the residual value or balloon payment. Lease payments are fully tax deductible to you as a business expense in many countries, but you will need to check with your own taxation jurisdiction to confirm tax deductibility in your country.

I find that this is a more effective way of managing the purchase of assets in your business.

Leases are standard practice in business and are generally easy for a small business owner to obtain. The key is demonstrating to the finance company that your business can afford the monthly lease payments based on the positive cash flow in your business.

In all leases the asset is used as security against the lease, so if your business was to default on the lease, the finance company would repossess the asset.

Leases can be quite flexible to suit a business's requirements. The influencing factors are the interest rate applied to the lease, the term of the lease, and the amount of the residual payment. The higher the monthly payments, the less the residual payment is and vice versa. It is better not to have a large residual payment at the end of the lease as the asset will generally not be worth the amount of the residual payment.

 Consider whether your business can utilise leasing as a way of purchasing business assets.

Hire Purchase

Hire purchase is similar to leasing, but with some key differences. With hire purchase the business owns the asset and not the finance company. The finance company is merely providing the debt for your business to purchase the asset, which means at the end of the agreement there is no residual/balloon payment as the asset already belongs to the business.

From a business accounting point of view, rather than paying a monthly lease payment to the finance company, the small business claims the interest cost of the hire purchase through the finance company. And because the small business owns the asset, it can claim depreciation. Hire purchase arrangements are set up so that there are often larger payments made to the finance company at the start of the agreement, and they get smaller towards the end of the agreement.

There can also be other tax benefits from hire purchase agreements. Consult with your accountant as they vary from country to country.

> **Consider if a hire purchase agreement is a viable option for your business when you need to purchase business assets.**

Business Loans and Repayments

At various times in the life of a small business, loans from a bank or finance company become necessary to fund growth. Business loans are usually secured by the business or the personal assets of the small business owner. The loan from the bank will often be a standard bank loan or a line of revolving credit. By talking to your accountant, you can determine the best option for your business.

If your business chooses to take a business loan over a fixed term at a certain interest rate, then it is often tempting for a business to pay the loan off when there is surplus cash in the business. Unless there is a really compelling reason to do so, like being charged exorbitant interest rates by the bank, then from a cash flow point of view it is highly unwise to repay the loan early.

Cash crises can occur at any time in a business life cycle, often due to reasons beyond the control of the business owner — think about the global markets crashing in 2008 and how many businesses were impacted. If all of a sudden your business needs cash, and it is not available because you repaid your loan, then the business will need to re-apply for another business loan to survive, and depending on the market and how your business is trading at the time, you may or may not get the financing.

It is safer for your business to pay off the loan each month according to the agreement and keep the cash in the bank for a rainy day.

Getting Through a Cash Flow Crisis

At some point, most businesses experience a negative cash flow. It can be a scary time for the business owner, but there are measures you can put in place to address the situation and turn your cash flow back into positive. There are eight key methods to address negative cash flow.

1. **Reduce the cash tied up in the business's operating cycle**
   As we explored earlier, accounts receivable and inventory holding can be major drains on cash flow. In a crisis situation, it is key that the business owner reduces the money held in accounts receivable by assertively collecting outstanding customer payments. At the same time, the business owner must increase the inventory turn so that there is less cash tied up in inventory in the business.

2. **Review and increase the business's gross profit margins**
   Essentially, this means either increasing the sales price of the products and services sold or reducing the cost of producing the goods (cost of goods sold).

3. **Reduce the operating expenses within the business**
   A business often incurs too many expenses for its size. With serious attention a business owner can heavily reduce expenses and therefore improve cash flow.

4. **Reduce sales volumes**
   By reducing the sales volumes, by default, sales and the cost of goods sold will decline. As a result, inventory holding will decline as will the money tied up in accounts receivable. This method of

cash flow control is difficult for small businesses to implement and, if undertaken for a considerable period, will require the business owner to substantially reduce operating expenses. This should be considered as an emergency response only.

5. Ask suppliers for extended payment terms

Delaying creditor payments needs to be a short-term solution for managing a negative cash flow as it can affect a business's credit rating with its suppliers. Holding back on the payment of inventory and other operating expenses will have a positive impact on cash flow. Delaying payment of invoices is illegal in some countries, so a better option is to proactively ask your supplier for extended credit terms to help your business through the cash flow crisis.

6. Borrow money

Borrowing money from banks, family or friends can help a business through short or long-term cash flow crises.

7. Find equity capital

If the cash crisis is ongoing, another option for a business is to find an equity partner who will contribute cash in exchange for a percentage of the business. This is fraught with danger if the wrong equity partner is found, as things can go very wrong in the business. Equally, it can be a real opportunity if the equity partner is genuinely interested in helping the business grow and become more profitable and successful. When considering this option, make sure your business gets the correct business advisory support to ensure the deal is not too one-sided in favour of the new equity partner.

8. Hold cash reserves

This is the pie-in-the-sky option for businesses existing hand to mouth each month and unable to amass cash reserves at the bank. Regardless, the only way in which a business will be less impacted by negative cash flows is to have a cash reserve. The best way to have a reserve is to put a bit of money aside for a rainy day during good times. I can promise you that after your business experiences a few nightmarish cash flow crises, you will never want it to happen again, so finding money to put aside for the future is the best way to protect the business for the future.

Adèle McLay, the Agitator
There you have it. My top strategies to ensure your cash flow is consistently positive. As I stressed previously, reading is one thing, implementation is another, so which of the strategies are you going to implement to enhance the cash flow in your business?

Strategies for Managing Cash Flow

Strategy 1

Take Control of Your Accounts Receivables Processes

There are some very simple but highly effective systems and processes that every small business can implement to improve the receipt of money owing from customers. The direct benefit of implementing some or all of these tools is that you will have substantially improved cash flow in your business, which will remove a lot of stress from you, the busy business owner.

Strategy 2

Take Control of Your Accounts Payable Processes

Accounts payable is a key area in which a business can positively affect its cash flow, so special attention needs to be paid to this part of the business too.

Strategy 3

Take Control of Your Inventory Levels and Inventory Turns

It may seem that all this 'stuff' about inventory and inventory turn is a bit technical, and I have to be honest and say, "Yes, that is true." However, if this is an area where you are not confident or do not have time to consider, your accountant should be retained to help you out. By effectively managing your inventories at appropriate levels, the cash flow in your business will be positively impacted, which helps you, the small business owner, to effectively manage your business success.

Strategy 4

Consider all the Options When Purchasing Business Assets

There is no right or wrong, better or worse way to approach financing business assets. Some business owners will prefer leasing while others will prefer hire purchase as they don't have to make a residual payment at the end of the lease. The key is to talk the options through with your accountant and to work out the numbers for leasing and hire purchase, and consider how they impact your business. Whatever you do, don't pay cash when paying for business assets.

Strategy 5

Keeping Cash in the Bank

Don't spend your cash repaying bank or finance company debt unless there is a compelling reason to. Ensure your business cash flows are maintained and use the cash reserves to cover emergency cash flow issues.

Andy Harrington

World Leading Public Speaking Expert and Trainer

Some would say that Andy Harrington lives a dream life. With his family he travels the world, speaking on stage with some of the world's leading business and motivational speakers who have included: Sir Richard Branson, Donald Trump, Bill Clinton, Tony Robins, and Brendon Burchard, to name a few. Andy is a public speaking entrepreneur, teaching public speaking from the stage, and selling entry to his *Public Speakers University* courses. He has developed a system that, when applied by his students, means they become expert public speakers.

But it hasn't always been that easy. Prior to establishing this, his third business, Andy suffered the financial failure of his second business due to a flawed business model. But as Andy says, you have to "lick your wounds and get back into the game". He returned with a more robust business model for this business, and as a result it has thrived. In establishing his current business, Andy was concerned not to 'overtrade' as he has the ability to grow businesses extraordinarily quickly. He has ensured this business growth is measured and has implemented an appropriate infrastructure to support the growth. Key to that infrastructure is a team of skilled staff.

One of the keys to the success of Andy's public speaking business is personal branding. Careful management of his personal brand has resulted in large promoters who organise international conferences now seeking Andy out and promoting him around the world. As he teaches communications to his audience, Andy has invested heavily in video technology to support the growth of his brand by enabling his audience to watch him via YouTube and to receive free tutoring if they opt-in to his free information. If they are interested, they can then pay to attend his training programmes. To achieve a worldwide audience, Andy has focused on dominating the YouTube categories of 'public speaking' and 'presentation skills', which gives him a competitive advantage.

Andy has also created modules and systems with his products, so that others on his team can teach the public speaking tools he has developed. Through doing that, he now has a scalable business that can grow without being totally reliant on him. Andy also has a business mentor who helps to flesh out ideas, acts as a sounding board, and challenges him in areas where his skills are weaker in business.

Andy's three key points for a budding entrepreneur are: 1) To be successful, an entrepreneur needs to specialise and stand out in some way. 2) Build a systematic business right from the very beginning, so that the business is not reliant on the entrepreneur. 3) Build winning teams around the business, advice Andy himself took from Sir Richard Branson.

Over the next six years Andy plans to exit from his business as a regular speaker, only appearing in selected elite events. To achieve that goal he will be focusing on finding and training the best speakers in the world to run the business and to teach the people who enrol on his public speaking training courses.

Adèle's Note: Notwithstanding some early business setbacks, Andy has always wanted to be an entrepreneur, so in establishing his public speaking business he learnt from his earlier mistakes, developed a clear vision and system for teaching public speaking, created a business infrastructure, and used his personal brand to grow his business. Today he is hugely successful, and 'brand' Andy Harrington is recognised and followed by vast numbers of people around the world. Andy is a truly inspiring professional speaker and teacher, and successful business man, who has found his niche and is reaping the rewards of his hard work.

To connect with Andy Harrington:
W: www.andyharrington.com
FB: Andy Harrington
YT: Andy Harrington

Entrepreneur Profile

Chapter 3

Actively Managing Your Business Expenses

> Drive thy business, let not that drive thee.
> **Benjamin Franklin**

As I said in Chapter One, my total focus in writing this book is to help your business make more profit and cash so you and your family can live the lifestyle you desire.

There are only two ways in which a business can make more profit:

- Increasing sales.
- Reducing expenses.

In this chapter, we look at business expenses; an area that often gets overlooked when considering how to improve the financial performance of a business.

Consider the following example, where gross income is $100, expenses are $70, and net profit before tax is $30. It doesn't matter whether we are talking thousands or millions, the principle is the same.

Let's say we want to double the net profit before tax in the business. If that is so, there are two ways to achieve that goal. We need to increase income or reduce expenses to double the profit. Table 3a demonstrates the simple options to double profit.

	Current Profit $	Doubling Income $	Reducing Expenses $
Gross Income	100	200	100
Less Expenses	-70	-140	-40
Net Profit Before Tax	30	60	60

Table 3a: Doubling Profit in Business

Looking at the options, we have $100 in gross income, and $30 in profit, which means expenses are $70. If we focus on growing the income alone, to double our profit to $60, with all other things being equal, we will need to double our income to $200, and corresponding expenses will increase to $140 in order to make the profit of $60.

Now let's look at expenses and assume that income is going to stay the same.

If we want to double our profit to $60 while keeping income at $100, then we need to reduce our expenses from $70 to $40. If we are able to achieve that result, then we have managed it by reducing our expenses by 43 percent (30 divided by 70).

Comparing the options, which might be easier to achieve in your business? A 100 percent increase in income/sales, or a 43 percent reduction in expenses?

While I accept that this example is very simple, it is designed to make the point that when businesses only focus on growing profit by increasing income, they miss an important element to their business—reducing expenses. There are often what I call 'low hanging fruit' in expenses that can be easily reduced to have a substantial impact on increasing profit.

In my experience as a business coach and consultant, I have often observed that business owners do not have a good understanding of the expenses their business incurs. They pay the bills but don't always consider how much they are spending in certain areas relative to the size of their business. Beyond that, the small business owner typically only gets their financial accounts prepared at the end of the year for tax purposes and by then it is too late to make any changes for the year that has already passed. Plus, small business owners spend most of their time on the day to day running of their business and don't think about their financials. It becomes a vicious cycle, with the small business owner never having control on a month by month basis of the financial transactions flowing through their business.

Common Sizing Your Financials

Let's look at another example. While I have simplified the numbers for this exercise, this is the essence of a real business I have worked with. The owner of this business, let's call her Mary, wanted to increase her profits by focusing on growing the business. Table 3b is a simplified summary of events over three years for Mary's business.

	Year 1 $(000)	Year 2 $(000)	Year 3 $(000)
Gross Profit	100	120	150
Less Expenses			
Staff	40	50	55
Travel	10	20	24
Stationery	2	5	7
IT	2	4	6
Entertainment	5	6	7
Other	1	3	4
Total Expenses	60	88	103
Net Profit Before Tax	**40**	**32**	**47**

Table 3b: Mary's Financial Information over Three Years

In Year 1, the gross profit (gross income less cost of goods sold) was $100,000; Year 2's gross profit was $120,000, a 20 percent increase; and in Year 3, gross profit was $150,000, a 50 percent increase from Year 1. On the face of it, the business owner would be happy with the 50 percent gross profit increase in her company. Mary thought by focusing on increasing sales/income, she would get a corresponding increase in profit. But that's not necessarily the case.

In this situation, Mary found that in Year 1 her net profit before tax as a percentage of gross profit in year 1 was 40 percent.

To calculate net profit as a percentage of gross profit, divide net profit before tax by gross profit.

Putting this calculation to work for the three years of the business, we find the following:

	Calculation	Net Profit Before Tax as a Percentage of Gross Profit
Year 1	40/100	40.0 percent
Year 2	32/120	26.7 percent
Year 3	47/150	31.3 percent

Table 3c: Net Profit Before Tax as a Percentage of Gross Profit

Mary was staggered at these results, which showed that despite growing her gross profits over two years, her net profits as a percentage of gross profit had decreased. In Year 1, her percentage return was 40 percent; Year 2, it was 26.7 percent, and in Year 3, it was 31.3 percent. Mary's business profit had declined notwithstanding the substantial growth in her gross profit.

It was at this point that I met Mary. Together, we took a closer look at what was really happening in her business.

Mary and I restated all the numbers in the business over the last three years to include percentages according to a template I gave her. Table 3d provides a summary of the financial information for the three years after we had done the exercise.

	Year 1 $(000)	Year 1 %	Year 2 $(000)	Year 2 %	Year 3 $(000)	Year 3 %
Gross Profit	100	100	120	100	150	100
Less Expenses						
Staff	40	40	50	41.7	55	36.7
Travel	10	10	20	18.3	24	16.6
Stationery	2	2	5	2.5	7	2.7
IT	2	2	4	3.3	6	4.0
Entertainment	5	5	6	5.0	7	4.7
Other	1	1	3	2.5	4	4.0
Total Expenses	60	60	88	73.3	103	68.7
Net Profit Before Tax	40	40	32	26.7	47	31.3

Table 3d: Common Sizing Mary's Financial Information

In Table 3d we restated all expenses as a percentage of gross profit. For example, in Year 1, staff expenses were $40,000. As a percentage of gross profit they are 40 percent ($40,000/$100,000). In Year 2, staff expenses were 41.7 percent of gross profit ($50,000/$120,000) and in Year 3, staff expenses were 36.7 percent of gross profit ($55,000/$150,000), and so on.

Look at the travel expenses; they rose from 10 percent of gross profit in Year 1 to 18.3 percent and 16.6 percent in Years 2 and 3 respectively. IT expenses rose from 2 percent of gross profit in Year 1 to 3.3 percent and 4 percent in Years 2 and 3 respectively.

Mary's stationery expenses rose from 2 percent to 2.5 and 2.7 percent in Years 2 and 3 respectively. Perhaps that doesn't seem like much of an increase, but I can tell you from my own experience, there is a lot of money to be saved in stationery if it is monitored. In one of my companies, the stationery representative used to visit one of my offices and sweet talk the reception staff who would spend a lot of money on stationery unbeknownst to the office manager, who was based at another location.

Other expenses increased from 1 percent in Year 1 to 2.5 and 4 percent respectively in Years 2 and 3. The other expenses category is an accounting catch all, and can hide a multitude of sins and excessive spending if not monitored at the granular level.

It might seem logical that if Mary increased her gross profit by 50 percent her expenses would have to increase. In reality, her expenses *may* need to rise, but not necessarily so and not by significant percentages.

Mary and I delved into the detail of her financial accounts, working with her accountant, to really understand the nature of the expenses she had incurred over the three years, particularly the last two years as she grew the gross profit in her business.

Table 3e is a summary of what we discovered:

Expenses	Comments
Staffing	The $10,000 and $15,000 in incremental staff costs from $50,000 in Year 1 were overtime payments Mary was making to her staff. When we analysed why she was making overtime payments, we discovered that there were no fundamental reasons for the staff to work later, except that many of the processing operations of the business were inefficient, which caused staff to have to work longer hours. Once we sorted the processes in the business Mary's staff expenses decreased.
Travel	When challenged, Mary recognised that she and some of her team were travelling more, incurring increased costs, when in reality they could use technology more efficiently in managing relationships with clients. Mary had a romantic notion attached to travelling in her business, feeling that she was more successful if she travelled more, when in reality, she was just wasting her money.
Stationery	There were no logical reasons why the stationery expenses were so high other than too much stationery being bought and held for future use. While the numbers were small, there was excessive spending in this area that could be better monitored.
Information Technology	Mary found that in tripling her IT expenses from $2,000 to $6,000, she had not gotten any greater technological efficiencies in her business, and that the company was just adding IT 'bits and pieces' here and there to keep up with the times. She agreed to review this area of her business.
Entertainment	Mary's business does require her to entertain clients from time to time, but when challenged, Mary conceded that entertainment is a nice-to-have expense, rather than an absolute essential to her winning and retaining clients, so she undertook to review company policies in relation to entertainment.
Other	In looking at the detail of 'Other Expenses', Mary and I found some savings, albeit small, to be made in this category.

Table 3e: Summary of Mary's Expenses Increases

Throughout Year 4, I acted as a performance coach — Inspirator, Agitator, Motivator™ — to Mary in her business, supporting her to largely maintain gross profit but more importantly, to actively manage all her business expenses. Table 3f demonstrates our achievement with this business strategy in Year 4.

	Year 1 $(000)	Year 1 %	Year 2 $(000)	Year 2 %	Year 3 $(000)	Year 3 %	Year 4 $(000)	Year 4 %
Gross Profit	100	100	120	100	150	100	140	100
Less Expenses								
Staff	40	40	50	41.7	55	36.7	45.0	32.1
Travel	10	10	20	18.3	24	16.6	12.0	8.6
Stationery	2	2	5	2.5	7	2.7	1.5	1.0
IT	2	2	4	3.3	6	4.0	2.5	1.8
Entertainment	5	5	6	5.0	7	4.7	3.5	2.5
Other	1	1	3	2.5	4	4.0	4.0	2.9
Total Expenses	60	60	88	73.3	103	68.7	68.5	48.9
Net Profit Before Tax	40	40	32	26.7	47	31.3	71.5	51.1

Table 3f: Mary's Financial Information after Four Years

As shown in Table 3f, gross profit in Year 4 was slightly reduced from Year 3 at $140,000, but with active management of Mary's business expenses, they ended up being 48.9 percent of gross profit, so that net profit before tax was $71,500 or 51.1 percent of gross profit. So not only was Mary continuing to enjoy increased gross profit, her net profit was also significantly higher, meaning she was able to pay herself more in the future if she continued to actively manage her business financials, particularly her business expenses.

Mary was delighted and determined to actively manage expenses in her business going forward so that regardless of how much her gross profit increased, she had full control of her expenses at all times, and therefore could maximise the increased gross profit, turning as much as possible into net profit before tax.

While I have simplified the numbers in Mary's business to demonstrate what we achieved, I hope it has prompted you to look at your business expenses as a percentage of gross profit. After doing that exercise, I can almost guarantee that you will find unnecessary expenses in your business. If you manage your costs more tightly, you will see a marked increase in your net profit before tax.

Ask your accountant to help you with this exercise by restating all your expenses as a percentage of gross income. If your accountant doesn't understand what you are talking about, show them this book. If your accountant doesn't think you need to do this exercise, get another accountant — quickly. They are probably a financial accountant and not a management accountant.

Financial accountants report on what has occurred in your business after the event, mostly at year end, unless you have quarterly or more frequent periodic accounts prepared. While annual accounts are important, they are an historic moment in time and are only useful to work out how much tax is owed.

A management accountant actively works with your business to help you understand the numbers in your business so you can focus on financial performance improvement.

Don't procrastinate about getting a new accountant if you feel that you should get one (I am allowed to say that as I trained as a chartered accountant). There are plenty out there in the market. Just make sure you move to an accountant who understands and supports you throughout the year with management accounting information.

Living Through Your Business

Let me give you another example of how often owners do not understand what is really happening in their business.

A client in the services industry I'll call Richard asked, "I have a great business. My turnover is excellent, but where is the money? I have little to show for it."

Using the common sizing of the financials as I described earlier, we learnt a lot about his business. Richard is a very successful marketing consultant and writer; he travels the world in business class for his work and lives a life that many envy. He dresses in the best brands, eats at the best restaurants, has a wine cellar many top restaurants would envy; his children attend private schools, and he has a nanny who accompanies the family when they travel internationally. Yet, Richard was concerned that his business profit was insufficient and wanted to understand why.

Table 3g shows two years of summarised and simplified financial information to demonstrate Richard's situation.

	Year 1 $(000)	Year 1 %	Year 2 $(000)	Year 2 %
Gross Profit	500	100	750	100
Less Expenses				
Staff (excl Richard's Drawings)	100	20	150	20.0
Travel and Accommodation	70	14	100	13.3
Entertainment	50	10	90	12.0
Motor Vehicles	20	4	25	3.3
Office	30	6	40	5.3
Other	90	18	130	17.3
Net Profit Before Tax	**140**	**28**	**215**	**28.8**

Table 3g: Richard's Financial Information over Three Years

On the face of it, it seems that Richard's business is successful. In Year 1, his gross profit was $500,000 and in Year 2, it was $750,000. As well, he has achieved net profit before tax of $140,000 and $215,000 in Years 1 and 2 respectively. Who wouldn't be happy with that?

Let's take a closer look at expenses. What do you notice? You may not notice much by looking at the pure numbers and percentages as they are fairly consistent between the two years. In actual fact, there are many issues with Richard's business, and it is not until one reviews the numbers more closely that the reality of Richard's business and lifestyle become obvious.

First, between Years 1 and 2, Richard's gross profit had gone up by 50 percent, yet his net profit was still around 28-29 percent. Over the same period of time, all of his business expenses increased in dollar terms, but as percentages of gross profit they remained largely the same. Richard was confused.

Together we analysed the financial numbers and percentages for all line items in his business, and then we delved into the detail of what expenses he was incurring within each expense item. As a result of that mammoth exercise, Richard learnt a big lesson in business and in life.

As well as incurring too many excessive expenses in his business, Richard was charging a lot of his personal living expenses to his business, and that was undermining the overall profitability of the business. While Richard did have a highly successful business, his lifestyle was too expensive and was impacting the financial success of his business.

Without going into the detail of all the issues, Table 3h summarises the key financial issues Richard had to make cold hard business decisions about.

Expenses	Comments
Staffing **Expenses increased by 50 percent**	• Substantially increased bonuses paid to key staff. • Overtime paid to support staff working late due to Richard being overseas and needing their support out of hours. • When travelling with family, Richard paid the nanny's wages and overtime payments from the business as the nanny was on call 24/7 for the children.
Travel and Accommodation **Expenses increased by 43 percent**	• Various members of Richard's staff also travelled with him, and were treated to business class tickets and expensive hotels. It was questionable whether Richard needed to travel with so many staff.

	• When travelling as a family, they consistently stayed in top class hotels, hiring a minimum of two to three rooms for the family alone, including a room for the nanny.
Entertainment **Expenses increased by 80 percent**	• Richard's staff were given substantial business expense accounts for entertainment, which they used regularly. • When travelling, the staff had unlimited bar tabs in the evenings and dined with Richard at high end restaurants. • Richard regularly paid for family meals out on his business credit cards. • Richard entertained clients and potential clients regularly when travelling and when at home, hosting them at top restaurants. • Richard paid for his personal wine collection through his business, and also purchased an extensive wine collection for his business for in-house entertaining. • Several family holidays abroad were paid for with the business's credit card.
Motor Vehicles **Expenses increased by 25 percent**	• Richard leased two very high-end cars; one for himself and one for his wife who did not work in the business. • The company paid for the car running costs for the nanny. • Richard also paid for the running costs of his classic car through the business.
Office **Expenses increased by 33 percent**	• Office expenses were considered to be within reason, although Richard undertook to review all line items for purchasing efficiency and to tighten the process of authorising office expenses.
Other **Expenses increased by 44 percent**	• Expenses included the corporate wardrobe costs for Richard, some key staff, and his wife, who bought at least one outfit for corporate entertaining each month. Most purchases were with high end named brands. • Richard had made considerable donations to charities that his family had connections with from the company account. The donations were in the form of sponsorships.

Table 3h: Richard's Business Expense Issues

Richard has an expensive lifestyle and an excessively expensive business. Richard was shocked at how much of his lifestyle was being paid for by his business. Most of the expenses are legitimate business expenses, but they were excessive and could be substantially reduced to ensure the business was more profitable.

I see this issue time and time again. Business owners complain that there is not enough profit in their business. Yet, when we strip back the numbers, the business is often fundamentally profitable when the personal living expenses are removed from it.

All business owners are entitled to charge some of their personal expenses through the business if the expense incurred is necessary for the creation of income. However, it is very easy to pull out the business credit card and charge many more expenses than necessary, resulting in the appearance of limited profitability.

Warren Buffet, the legendary investor, has two excellent quotes that are relevant here.

On spending: "If you buy the things you do not need, soon you will have to sell the things that you do need."

On saving: "Do not save what is left after spending, but spend what is left over after saving."

Adèle McLay, the Agitator

Common sizing your financials is a great way to fully understand what is occurring in your business, and how efficiently your business is being managed. But, it takes time and effort and will likely require the support of your accountant to enable you to fully understand what is happening from a financial point of view. Are you ready to do the work, and see exactly how well your business is operating?

Strategy 6

Take Control of Your Business Expenses

Focusing on reducing expenses cannot be the only way in which you grow the profit in your business. However, once you have control of your expenses then you have a strong platform to consider other ways to grow your profits, including growing sales.

Common sizing your financials is an excellent tool to gain total control of your business expenses. The key to achieving control is having monthly management accounts prepared for you by your accountant, so you can analyse your business's financial performance, tweaking things as necessary to achieve Big Profits.

Veronica Pullen

Social Marketing Queen

Imagine having Asperger's Syndrome, rheumatoid arthritis, hearing difficulties, an eyesight issue which means you are blind at night, and mobility issues. What might life hold for you? Meet Veronica Pullen. She has all those health issues, but that hasn't stopped her being a hugely successful entrepreneur based in the United Kingdom. Because of her ailments, Veronica began networking online 18 years ago; through internet chat rooms and forums, she made friends. A book keeper by day, online networker by night, Veronica realised that business people were starting to wonder how to use the online world to network – something she had been doing for years. So, a new social media business was born.

Veronica admits she did undertake some social media training, but soon realised she knew as much as the trainers. What she needed to learn was how to build and run a business to support her social media skill set. Veronica is passionate about learning, so even today, while running a hugely successful business, she is continuing to explore new ways to develop and run her business.

At first Veronica tried to ignore her health challenges, thinking that if she just focused on her expertise in social media, no one would pay any attention to her health issues. She was wrong. By not acknowledging her issues, Veronica found she alienated her audience. Once she began to 'weave in' her health challenges, people started to accept her as they respected the personal challenges she had overcome, and continues to overcome to this day.

As you might expect, being a social marketing queen, Veronica has built her customer base via social media. The friends she had developed became her first customers when she established her new business, and in turn they continue to refer her to their friends. Now Veronica has social media customers all over the world, and some very well known names have their social media activity managed by Veronica and her team.

Veronica has been shortlisted for and won various business awards. She credits a lot of her business success to having mentors and coaches supporting her. They teach her and she always implements their teachings. She also continues to participate in Mastermind type coaching groups with others in business. These environments ensure Veronica continues down the right path in her business. Veronica's greatest joy in business is that she owns and runs a business that is an extension of herself. As she says, she "shows up as Veronica"! She gets paid to talk about and teach the things she lives for. For Veronica, there is no distinction between work and play. It is all play!

To be successful in business, Veronica believes: 1) Do something in business that you love. If you are not passionate about it, you will not achieve the success you aspire to achieve. 2) Always make sure you are networking with people who are more successful than you. If you want to grow your business, look at the people who are around you, and make sure they are helping you to go forward and not holding you back. 3) That all businesses need to embrace the power of social media to support the growth of their business.

Adèle's Note: Veronica is amazing. She decided early on that she would not let her health issues affect the quality of her life, and she hasn't. Veronica has embraced her ailments, and has used them to her advantage. She has a hugely successful international business, and aspires to achieve even more. She has set herself some significant goals for the next five years, and is on track to achieve them. Veronica has found that she enjoys the life of a celebrity and being recognised, so has set her sights on presenting her material on the stage to larger groups of people. Go Veronica. You are an inspiration.

To connect with Veronica Pullen:
W: www.veronicapullen.co.uk
FB: Veronica M Pullen
YT: Veronica Pullen
Tw: @veronicapullen

Chapter 4

Where Do Your Profits Come From?

> More business is lost every year through neglect than through any other cause. **Rose F Kennedy**

In Chapter Three, we focused on expenses and ensuring you have full control during the year of the expenses your company incurs. By fully controlling your business expenses — only spending what you have to rather than what you want to — your business will see a tremendous improvement in profitability and cash flow.

Remember, there are two ways to make more profit in a business:

- Increasing sales.
- Reducing expenses.

In this chapter, we look at increasing sales. In my experience most small businesses just get out into the market and promote all their products and services to existing and potential customers in the hope that they buy more with little thought about the impact that selling strategy has on the business's profitability.

I call it the scatter gun approach. While it will work for a period, the business owner is not targeting profitable customers with profitable products and service offerings, so from a financial point of view the business is often wasting opportunities and getting the scraps of business that comes their way. It is not a winning strategy to success in business.

The net result is the business is not as successful as the business owner dreamed it would be, and they are often working all hours to make money, so the return on investment on their time is negligible. This is no way to run a successful business.

Most businesses sell more than one product or service. Seldom do I see a business that understands which of their products or services actually make the business money or make the most money. When properly analysed, most businesses will have products or services that make a loss or are only marginally profitable for the business.

My sole objective in this chapter is to ensure that your business sells loads of the products or services that make the most amount of money. There are some fundamental accounting principles in business that, as a business owner or manager, you need to understand to get the most financial success from your business: *gross margin* and *gross margin analysis*.

Say your business has 10 products or services that it sells, and in any one year you can only sell a maximum of 1,000 of those products or services. Would you want to sell your most profitable products or services to your customers in order to maximise the gross profit into your business? The answer should be yes.

Gross Margin

Gross margin is a very exciting and enlightening tool in business, but sadly, it is not widely understood. Similarly, many accountants do not fully appreciate the value of undertaking *gross margin analysis* for their customers because most only prepare year end accounts for tax purposes and not periodic management accounts that would enable the business owner to understand and work on the financial performance of their business.

Gross margin is a business tool that helps you to work out which of your products and services make the most amount of gross profit for your business.

If business owners do not understand gross margin, they will miss out on opportunities to maximise their business's gross profit. Plus, by understanding gross margin, you can also impact your business's cash flow. If you are selling your most profitable products and services, then once payment is collected, your business will enjoy greater positive cash flow, all other things being equal.

Business profits are maximised when the business is selling its most profitable products and services to its most profitable customers.

Some of the key benefits when using gross margin include:

- The most and least profitable products and services are identified.
- It helps make decisions about removing unprofitable products and services from the business.
- The most and least profitable customers are identified.
- It helps make decisions to 'resign' from least profitable customers.
- The information can be used to profit plan the business each year.
- It enables the business owner to make comparisons on the financial performance of their business relative to industry averages and competitors.
- It helps improve business profitability and cash flow, leading to the business owner having more disposable income to fund their lifestyle.

Gross margin is a simple calculation, but a full understanding of it can have a fundamental impact on the profitability of your business. Gross margin can be represented as a dollar amount or as a percentage. In both instances, the calculations are very simple.

$$\text{Gross margin as a percentage} = \frac{\text{Sales Price} - \text{Cost of Goods Sold}}{\text{Sales Price}}$$

$$\text{Gross margin in dollars} = \text{Sales Price} - \text{Cost of Goods Sold}$$

The gross margin percentage is the sale price for your product or service minus the total of all the costs associated with producing that product or service, divided by the sales price. Or even simpler, the dollar gross margin is sales price minus the cost of goods sold.

At times, gross margin and gross profit are used interchangeably, but they are not the same, as I will explain later.

The cost of goods sold is also known in accounting terms as direct costs or variable costs and are made up of all the costs that a business incurs when buying, manufacturing, and preparing products or services for sale.

Examples of cost of goods sold include:

- For manufactured goods: cost of goods sold are all the variable costs that are incurred in manufacturing the products, including all raw materials and labour costs of the manufacturing staff.
- For retailers: the cost of goods sold is the variable inventory costs incurred.
- For service businesses: cost of goods sold is more difficult to define and is industry specific. Variable costs could include commissions paid to sales staff and costs associated with hiring equipment to complete a job.

To ease you into the concept of gross margins, let me give you a simple example. Let's assume you have a product you sell for $120 and the variable/direct costs to selling that product are $50, meaning the cost of goods sold is $50. Therefore the profit on that product is $70. Table 4a depicts this simple calculation.

Gross Margin Calculation	$
Product Sales Price	120
Less Product Cost of Goods Sold	-50
Product $ Gross Margin	**70**
Product Gross Margin Percentage	**58.30%**

Table 4a: Calculation of Gross Margin

In the Table 4a example, the gross margin for the product is 58.3 percent:

$$\frac{120 - 50}{120} = 58.3 \text{ percent}$$

And the dollar gross margin is $70 ($120 − $50).

When gross margin is referred to as a percentage, we would say that the product had a 58.3 percent gross margin. This means that for every $100 of product sold, 58.3 percent of that sale makes a contribution to the gross profit.

At times we also refer to gross margin as a dollar number. In this instance the gross margin is $70, meaning a sale of one unit of this product makes a $70 contribution to gross profit. On its own, the dollar gross margin calculation is not very helpful, but when further analysed it becomes extremely useful in determining a business's most profitable products and services.

Just to confuse things, at times dollar gross margin is interchanged with the term gross profit. If this business only sold one product, then the dollar gross margin is also the gross profit per unit sold on that particular product, but most businesses are not like that.

In a business that sells lots of products or services, gross profit means something else: the total of all the gross margins of your products or services sold.

To explain further, let's assume you have three products in your business, and the gross margin of Product 1 is $50, Product 2 is $30, and Product 3 is $10. Table 4b shows the gross profit per product and the total gross profit.

Dollar sales of Product 1 total $120,000, on Product 2 sales are $160,000, and on Product 3 sales are $120,000. Sales per product are calculated by multiplying the sales price per unit by the number of units sold.

The gross profit on Product 1 is $100,000; on Product 2 gross profit is $120,000; and Product 3 has a gross profit of $60,000. Gross profit per product is calculated by multiplying the dollar gross margin by the number of units sold.

	Sales Price per Unit $	No. of Units Sold in a Year	Sales per Product $	Gross Margin per Product $	Gross Profit per Product $
Product 1	60	2,000	120,000	50	100,000
Product 2	40	4,000	160,000	30	120,000
Product 3	20	6,000	120,000	10	60,000
Total Gross Profit					280,000

Table 4b: Calculation of Gross Profit

The total gross profit for the business is $280,000 and that is calculated by adding the gross profits for all the products sold. Hopefully you can now clearly see that gross margin is different to gross profit. Most businesses are like this. They sell lots of different products and services in different volumes and with different gross margins, and therefore, different gross profits per product.

The information in Table 4b, while useful in telling us about product gross margin, gross profit and total gross profit, does not indicate how this business could increase sales in its most profitable products. Gross margin analysis will help determine which products and services are performing strongly or weakly.

> **Understand the fundamentals of the gross margins of your products and services, and all of a sudden you will think about your business differently.**

Gross Margin Analysis

Gross margin analysis determines which of your products or services makes the most gross profit. If we review Table 4b again, it might appear that Product 2 should be promoted more as it generates sales of $160,000 per annum compared to the other two, which generate $120,000 in sales annually.

However, if we look at the gross margins as a percentage, then things look a little different.

The gross margin percentage on Product 2 is 75 percent ($30/$40). For Product 3, it is 50 percent ($10/$20), and for Product 1, it is a massive 83 percent ($50/$60).

Remember for every $100 of sales the gross margin percentage shows how much is left over as a contribution to gross profit. So for Table 4b, for every $100 in sales of Product 1, it contributes $83.30 to gross profit; Product 2 contributes $75, and Product 3 contributes $50. Armed with this information, promoting Product 1 would have the biggest impact on gross profit.

When we look at some more numbers, it becomes clear. Let's assume the business could sell an extra 50 units of either Products 1, 2 or 3 in a year. Now that we know the gross margin percentage, we know for certain that Product 1 will contribute the most money to gross profit for each extra sale that is made.

As can be seen in Table 4c, in a perfect world this business would opt to sell more of Product 1 to maximise gross profit in the business. Using this example, Product 1 makes a $2,500 contribution to gross profit if 50 extra units are sold, whereas Product 2 contributes $1,500, and Product 3 contributes a mere $500.

	No. of Units Sold	Gross Margin $	Gross Profit Contribution per Product $
Product 1	50	50	2,500
Product 2	50	30	1,500
Product 3	50	10	500

Table 4c: Maximising Gross Profit

In a nutshell, that is gross margin analysis. Now that you have these tools, I hope you will quickly start reviewing all your products and services to determine their gross margins as dollar amounts and percentages so you know exactly what is occurring in your business and which of your products and services offer the greatest contribution to gross profit.

Now, very few businesses can pick the most profitable products and services and just sell them. There are often compelling reasons why less profitable products and services need to be part of the mix that are offered for sale.

However, knowledge is power, and by knowing the gross margins of all your products and services, you can then start profit planning for future years to ensure you sell the mix of products and services that maximises the gross profit in your business.

> **Gross margin analysis is a powerful tool for a business to use to maximise its profits by selling more of its most profitable products and services.**

Profit Planning

Profit planning is a nicer way of saying *forecasting your profit and loss statement*. It means creating a profit statement that plans for the forthcoming financial performance of your business. Once established, you can manage your business's actual performance against the plan to see how you are tracking each month, and at that time, tweak the activities of the business to keep on track to achieve the profit plan for the year.

Sound exciting? I do hope so. A business needs to understand the concepts of gross margin and gross profit to fully maximise the profitability of the business. By understanding the numbers, taking control of them, and using them to your advantage, your business will achieve its full potential.

Adèle McLay, the Agitator

Oh no, I can hear you say. She is about to ask me to do more number crunching!! Yes, you are right. By understanding the true profitability of your products and services, you can then use the information to determine the best combination of products and services to be selling in your business to generate maximum profit. Get your accountant to help you, but please get to grips with product and service profitability.

Strategy 7

Gross Margin Analysis Leads To Increased Product Profitability

Get to grips with Gross Margin Analysis for your products and services, and watch your business profits soar, as you will feel compelled to promote for sale the most profitable products and services on offer within your business.

Bice Awan

Social Entrepreneur, CEO – Skylight Trust

Skylight Trust, a non-governmental social enterprise, was established in 1997 in Wellington, New Zealand after key community leaders identified a lack of local and national resources to support children and adults who were experiencing stress, grief and trauma. Bice, who has a significant international health consulting background, took up the role of chief executive, and spearheaded the development of Skylight, which today is a leader in providing support and resources in New Zealand and across the world to people in desperate circumstances.

Bice started the Trust as a 'one-woman-band' and has grown it significantly on the back of a strong vision. Not without its own business challenges, even today, Bice notes, "that the Skylight Trust is still moving along the social enterprise continuum from dependency to total financial independence." "Social enterprise is a philosophy of balancing social missions with revenue generation, but we haven't got to the stage yet of being fully in that position." Bice commented that, "it is important never to lose sight of either in managing and growing the enterprise day-to-day."

To address the issue of financial independence, Bice and her team established a publishing arm to the enterprise, and to date have published over 50 resources, which are available for purchase. The resources are of such a high quality and relevancy, that Skylight Trust has won major organisational customers and contracts in New Zealand, Australia, Denmark and Saudi Arabia, to name a few countries.

Branding and marketing has played a key role in Skylight's development. Skylight sees itself as a 'hope broker'; it can't fix somebody's trauma, loss or grief, but Skylight can give hope for the future. This message is used strongly as part of its branding and marketing strategies.

On the back of the strong branding and marketing work, which has created significant visibility for Skylight, it enjoys significant repeat business with its customers, many of which are very large organisations seeking a holistic approach to working with grief, stress and trauma in their organisations.

To be successful in developing a social enterprise, Bice believes in: 1) Establishing a board of directors who truly understand the importance of balancing a social mission and financial imperatives. 2) Having working capital available from the beginning, as most enterprises don't and that is a real commercial challenge. 3) Developing profitable partnerships with other agencies as those associations can be very powerful and provide a way of growing a social enterprise in the early years.

Adèle's Notes: Bice's vision and drive to make a difference has been the cornerstone of Skylight's success as a social enterprise in New Zealand and internationally, in the lives of those affected by stress, grief and trauma, and whose voices are often not heard. As a leading Government official said to Bice, "If Skylight didn't exist, New Zealand would be a very sad place!" As well as being successful in achieving its social mission, Skylight as a business is a success. Recognising the need for financial independence, it has developed significant and profitable revenue streams which, as those continue to grow, will hopefully allow the enterprise to enjoy absolute financial security. Bice and this enterprise are a true inspiration for business owners and other social enterprise leaders.

To connect with Skylight and Bice Awan:
W: www.skylight.org.nz
Tw:@skylightNZ
FB: Skylight-Trust

Chapter 5

Who Are Your Most Profitable Customers?

> Business is all about solving people's problems - at a profit! **Paul Marsden**

I regularly ask my coaching clients the following three questions:

1. How many customers do you have?

2. Which customers are the most profitable for your business?

3. Which customers do you enjoy working with the most and why?

The last question is the easiest for my clients to answer because they can give me an emotional response rather than a fact-based response. The first two questions require analysis of their business, and most of my clients have usually not done that prior to meeting me.

Many businesses, accountants, and business coaches/consultants do not see the importance of measuring how many customers a business has and which ones are the most profitable. I see things totally differently and Question 2 is especially important in my opinion.

I find that most businesses I work with have never actively thought about the profile of the customer they would like for their business. Rather, they have an open door policy, where they will pitch their business to anyone who shows an interest. In many respects they are living hand to mouth and are grateful for any customers that come their way.

What is your approach to potential customers in your business? Do you grab them with open arms, discounting to get the business?

In order to achieve their full potential and to deliver the business success they are seeking, I believe that a business owner must value themselves and their business, and seek to work with the most appropriate and profitable customers rather than accept all and any customers into their business. In order to achieve this, a business must have a good understanding of the profitability of its products and services as we discussed in Chapter Four, as well as understanding, with existing customers, how profitable or otherwise they are.

In pondering this issue, I devised a four quadrant approach to customer profitability and management. I call it my *'L⁴ Customer Profitability Quadrant'*. L⁴ relates to the types of customers you have. They fall into four categories or quadrants in my system, being:

- 'Lose Them'
- 'Look Out'
- 'Lift Up'
- 'Lots More'

Think about it. Do you have customers where you should *'lose them'* or *'look out'* because of them, or *'lift up'* their importance within your business, or find *'lots more'* of the same types of customers for your business?

To understand the *L⁴ Customer Profitability Quadrant's* power in relation to your business will require spending a bit of time working out the numbers. You may need your accountant's assistance, but please try it to change the way in which you view your customers. It will also certainly help you to up-sell products to your best and most enjoyable customers, and seek out more of the types of customers you enjoy working with and which are highly profitable to your business.

First, you need to work out the profitability of every customer to your business. If you have a large number of customers, the chances are you have a fairly decent accounting system, and therefore the system should be able to do some of the work for you.

Second, you need to give each customer an enjoyment score between one and 10. This is totally subjective and really represents the emotional response you and your staff have towards individual customers. An enjoyment score of one means your business does not enjoy having this customer as they are difficult to deal with and can be rude, demanding, disloyal, uncooperative, or whatever other reason you don't enjoy having them buy from you.

If you rate your customer an enjoyment score of 10, this means you absolutely enjoy them as people, they are easy to deal with and are genuinely pleasing to service, loyal and a good customer to have within your business.

In order to accurately assess the enjoyment score your business has for your customers, it is important that you involve your staff in this exercise, as often they are the people at the coal face dealing with the customer on a day to day basis, whereas you as the business owner may be removed and therefore have a different enjoyment score that you ascribe to customers.

Table 5a depicts a business's view of its customers. Let's call them ABC Limited.

Customer	Customer Gross Margin	Enjoyment	Customer	Customer Gross Margin	Enjoyment
1	46	3	26	58	5
2	40	4	27	60	10
3	31	6	28	61	5
4	20	8	29	51	6
5	46	8	30	31	3
6	72	9	31	76	10
7	85	7	32	24	2
8	78	1	33	35	2
9	43	1	34	84	9
10	63	2	35	25	7
11	76	5	36	7	9

12	78	10	37	15	4
13	80	8	38	40	7
14	45	10	39	79	4
15	22	10	40	70	6
16	10	6	41	71	2
17	6	2	42	46	4
18	20	3	43	41	5
19	76	8	44	15	5
20	60	7	45	25	6
21	65	3	46	36	5
22	80	6	47	85	4
23	35	9	48	76	3
24	55	9	49	70	4
25	48	6	50	85	3

Table 5a: ABC Limited - L⁴ Customer Profitability Quadrant

The calculation to determine customer gross margin is similar to that of the product gross margin we discussed in Chapter Four.

$$\text{Customer Gross Margin} = \frac{\text{Total Customer Sales} - \text{COGS for Customer}}{\text{Total Customer Sales}} \times 100$$

So for instance, if Customer 24 buys $2000 of services in one year, and cost of goods sold is $900, then the equation is:

$$\text{Customer 24} = \frac{\$2000 - \$900}{\$2000} \times 100 = 55 \text{ percent}$$

For service based businesses it is often harder to determine COGS. In those situations, I recommend that COGS includes the staff costs (wages/overtime/bonuses) of those staff who directly service the customer.

Using my example above, the customer gross margin calculation means that with the combination of products and services sold to Customer 24, the gross margin is 55 percent. Another way of stating this is that for every $1000 of sales made to Customer 24, $550 contributes to the business's gross profit.

Now we plot all the customer profitability and enjoyment scores on the *L⁴ Customer Profitability Quadrant* as depicted in Table 5b. Take a look at where the customers fall on the quadrant. They are largely all over the place in this example, which is interesting to look at when depicted like this. My client had never done this exercise before and was shocked at the reality of his customer base when looking at it from a customer profitability and enjoyment point of view.

What might your customer profiles look like if you were to plot your customers onto the *L⁴ Customer Profitability Quadrant*?

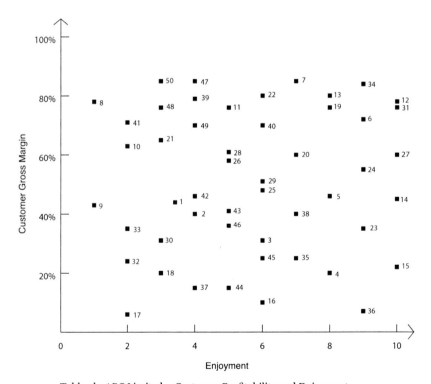

Table 5b: ABC Limited – Customer Profitability and Enjoyment

If we overlay my L⁴ quadrant across the grid, we start to build a picture of the customers, as depicted in table 5c. The quadrant is very simple. It simply slices the grid in half both ways. So you draw a line across at 50 percent profitability and a line down at an enjoyment score of 5.

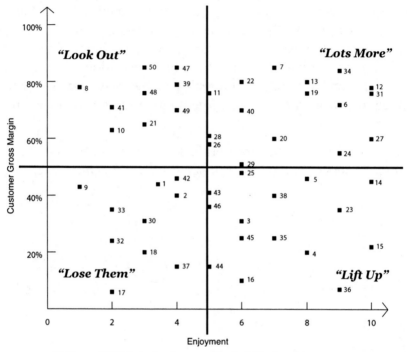

Table 5c: ABC Limited – Customer Profitability Quadrant

We can see that these customers are falling into four quadrants, or the L⁴ quadrants as I call them. What do the four quadrants represent?

In the bottom left quadrant are the customers that are low in profitability and enjoyment factor, so I call this the 'Lose Them' quadrant.

In the top left quadrant we have the highly profitable customers, but the enjoyment factor is low. I call this the 'Look Out' quadrant.

In the bottom right quadrant, we have customers that we really enjoy working with but they are not very profitable to the business. I call this the '*Lift Up*' quadrant.

In the top right quadrant, we have customers that are highly profitable and are highly enjoyable to work with. I call this the '*Lots More*' quadrant.

Take a minute to understand what the *L4 Customer Profitability Quadrant* is really telling us. This is really important for any business to understand. If we look at customer 34 on the quadrant, they are contributing 84 percent gross margin and the enjoyment factor within the business is 9 out of 10. A fantastic customer for any business to have!

Yet, if we look at customer 18 on the quadrant (almost the polar opposite of customer 34), they are contributing 20 percent gross margin and the enjoyment factor is 3 out of 10.

In simple terms, for every $1000 that customer 34 spends with the business, they contribute $840 towards the business's gross profit and are enjoyable to work with, whereas with customer 18, for every $1000 they spend, they contribute a meagre $200 towards gross profit and are difficult to work with.

If those were two customers in your business, which one would you prefer to work with more and want more of? The answer is simple. A successful business wants more customers like customer 34, and no customers like customer 18.

Unless this type of customer profitability analysis is done, your business will not know the composition of its customers, and could well be working with the wrong customers for your business, and therefore inhibiting your business success.

Now let's get down to the nitty gritty of what each customer type really represents in your business.

'Lose Them' Quadrant

I wonder how many businesses have customers that are really hard going and not very profitable to the business. This type of customer sucks the life out of the business, when business should largely be fun. Because this type of customer is difficult to work with, they will also often be time consuming to service. Having to work with customers that fall in this category is a waste of time and energy. That time and energy would be better spent working with enjoyable and profitable customers and finding more profitable customers for the business.

So why do businesses continue to work with this type of customer? Firstly, because they generally don't think about this type of customer in this way as most businesses have never undertaken any form of customer profitability/enjoyment analysis, and secondly, they don't think about the impact this type of customer is having on the business. Thirdly, if they do, the business is often fearful that losing a customer will have a negative impact on the business. After all, any customer is better than no customers, right? No.

So, what should you do with these customers? The clue is in the heading: lose them! Once you get over the emotional challenge of moving a customer on and realise by doing that you will have more time to focus on your better quality and more profitable customers, the method to achieve the departure of these customers is easy.

If you have competitors in your business that are local to the customer, I suggest you first make contact with the competitors and let them know that you are restructuring your business and as a result you now have a selection of customers that your business can no longer effectively service and that you would be delighted to pass over to them. Your competitors are likely to be delighted at the prospect of being handed some new customers and will no doubt respond positively.

Once that is done, you then write a very polite letter to your 'Lose Them' customers, explaining to them that your business has recently restructured and you are no longer able to effectively service their requirements. However, you do recommend other businesses (name them) and have made contact with those businesses, and they would be delighted to meet the customer and assist them in the future.

Easy. Job done respectfully and professionally to all parties. You have actively chosen to lose a customer. As Sir Alan Sugar says in the BBC series, *The Apprentice* — "You're fired." I bet you feel great at the thought. Now your business can focus on its other customers.

Having said all of that, there may be some of the customers in the *'Lose Them'* quadrant who are in the top right hand side of the quadrant that might warrant further analysis. They are bordering on contributing good profit to your business, yet the enjoyment factor is less than five. In those circumstances, I would be asking my clients to consider what issues they are experiencing with the customers in this section of the *'Lose Them'* quadrant. Depending on the answer, it may be worthwhile arranging a meeting with those customers to resolve any issues in order to improve the working relationship, and to enable more up-selling of services and products to take these customers to the lower section of the *'Lots More'* quadrant. If that is not able to be achieved then those customers get fired too!

'Look Out' Quadrant

Customers that sit in the *'Look Out'* quadrant are a challenge and risk to a business. They are profitable (and at times highly profitable), but they are not enjoyable to work with. As this is a high risk quadrant, personally I don't think any business should have too many customers sitting in it. Rather, they need to be moved to the *'Lots More'* quadrant or out of your business.

There is potentially a myriad of reasons why customers in the *'Look Out'* quadrant are difficult to work with. Because the customers in this quadrant are highly profitable, before deciding what to do with them, they need to be further analysed on a customer by customer basis.

The challenge for your business with these customers is the profit they contribute to your business, notwithstanding the low enjoyment factor. If these customers were to leave your business, it potentially results in a major impact on profitability. Yet, because the enjoyment factor is low, there is a real chance they may not be loyal to your business, so there is a flight risk; they could find another supplier at any time and therefore impact the turnover and profitability of your business.

If we take a closer look at the *'Look Out'* quadrant, we see in this example we have a number of customers that hover around the 4-5 mark for enjoyment, and they are at the upper end of profitability for the business. Table 5d depicts the customers that may be worth more attention. With those customers, we need to ask ourselves the questions:

- Why is the customer not enjoyable to work with? Be honest.
- Would a meeting with the customer potentially improve the enjoyment factor if the needs of the customer are better understood?

Once we have those answers then the strategy is clear. I am very much of the opinion that a business should attempt to fully understand the needs of its customers, and continually review those needs regardless of the enjoyment score they are given. There is usually a reason why relationships are challenged (be they personal or business), and it is often a mismatch of understanding around expectations and delivery.

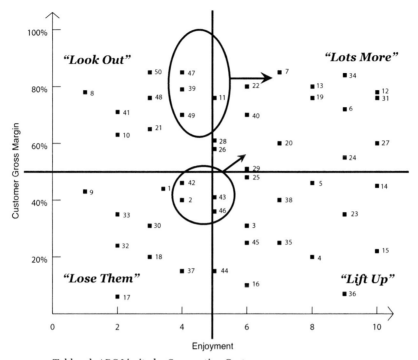

Table 5d: ABC Limited – Segmenting Customers

With the customers that fall into the top right hand side of the 'Look Out' quadrant, I recommend setting up a meeting between your business and the key people you deal with in their business to further understand what they need from your business, resolve any outstanding issues, and create a plan that supports developing a more enjoyable and productive working relationship. Often a lack of effective communication causes the problem, and this can easily be resolved.

Once a meeting has been held, both parties might find that there is an opportunity to change the way in which business is conducted, thereby enhancing the enjoyment factor in the relationship while maintaining or enhancing the profitability factor, thus moving those customers into the 'Lots More' quadrant.

For those customers in the 'Look Out' quadrant that cannot be moved to the 'Lots More', it is time to review the relationship with them, notwithstanding their profitability. If the relationship cannot be improved, perhaps they would be better served by a competitor, freeing you and your business up to work with your *'Lots More'* customers.

It is unlikely that a business will never have customers in the *'Look Out'* quadrant. My advice is to be careful and try to limit the volume of customers that sit there, otherwise your business could be financially compromised if the customer chooses to fire you and your business. That is always a possibility too!

'Lift Up' Quadrant

Customers in this *'Lift Up'* quadrant pose a quandary for your business. They are good customers to deal with and service, and are probably highly loyal to your business, yet they are not very profitable. Often, because these customers are good to deal with, your staff will 'over service' these customers as well, in order to maintain the interaction, because it is enjoyable. Hmmm, this behaviour needs to change within your business in order to improve customer profitability.

This is actually an easy dilemma to resolve and one that many businesses would like to have. These *'Lift Up'* customers are already wedded to your business, so given the opportunity, the chances are very high that they will want to buy more from your business. In Chapter Six we talk about cross selling, up selling, down selling and frequently selling. Those techniques are perfect for the *'Lift Up'* customers. Often customers are not aware of the full range of products offered by a business, or the business has not considered the full requirements of the customer in making offers. Depending on your business, the easiest way to address this situation is to find out more about what your customers do and what they might need from your business, and make offers.

You can find out this information by arranging meetings with the customers if your business suits that type of interaction, undertaking customer research, or inviting a group of customers to talk with you in a 'focus group' type situation.

On many occasions I have personally been invited to focus group meetings in order for a business to understand more about how they are perceived and what their customers might like from them. The best meeting of this kind I ever went to was while I was living and working in New Zealand. I was a regular customer on the national airline, Air New Zealand, and a member of Koru Club, the airline's frequent flyer member system. Through their research company, Air New Zealand invited members to come along and sample the food offerings they wanted to serve on their aeroplanes and in their lounges. Yum! It was a great experience for the customers who attended, and hopefully it was a productive exercise for the airline.

'Lots More' Quadrant

Well, these customers are your goldmines, and should be treated like kings and queens. They are highly profitable to your business, and they are enjoyable to work with.

The key here is to analyse what makes them enjoyable to work with: is it the company; the industry; the type of products and services they buy?

How do you usually get introduced to these types of customers? Is it by the advertising your business does? By introduction or referral? By cold calling on industries or companies you are keen to target?

Once you have analysed this for your business, then you can start working on targeting more of the same types of customers to your business using the marketing tools we talk about in Chapter Eight.

For the *'Lots More'* customers in the lower segment of the quadrant, because your business has a great relationship with the customer, you can now focus on continuing to up-sell them by understanding more of their business needs and how you can support them, a bit like what you will do for your customers in the *'Lift Up'* category.

Customer Profitability in Summary

Now you know how important it is to understand the composition of your customers from a customer profitability point of view. Once you have done this in your business, by focusing your business efforts on further understanding your customers' needs, and firing those that you cannot adequately service, your business profits will sky rocket.

Table 5e demonstrates how I challenge my clients to re-focus their existing customers in the various quadrants. Do this too, your profits will soar, and you will have fun working with and serving your enjoyable customers, both existing and the new ones you will target.

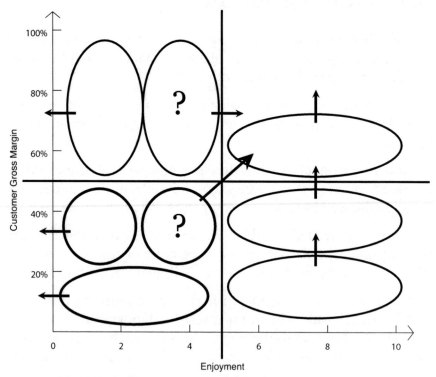

Table 5e: The Perfect L⁴ Customer Profitability Quadrant

Adèle McLay, the Agitator

I just love my L^4 *Customer Profitability Quadrant* because once a business clearly understands where all its customers sit on the quadrant, the business owner can take charge of their business in order to maximise profitability, and importantly, the enjoyment experienced with customers. If there is one thing only that you take from this book, I would ask you to take this. Analyse your customer base and see what happens, and notice how you feel about your business when you see the quadrant in relation to your business. I believe you will want to make changes in the composition of your customer base to have as many customers as possible in the 'Lots More' quadrant.

 Strategy 8

Customer Profitability is Critical to Improving your Business Profits

Fully understand the dynamics of your customer profitability profiles. Once understood, implement strategies to:

- Sell more to your most profitable and enjoyable customers – your 'Lots More' customers.
- Find new customers that will naturally fall into your 'Lots More' quadrant.
- Up-sell to your less profitable but enjoyable customers – your 'Lift Up' customers.
- Improve the business relationship with your highly profitable but unenjoyable customers or fire them – your 'Look Out' customers.
- Remove or improve your unenjoyable and low profitability customers – your 'Lose Them' customers.

Shannon Lea Reynolds

Consultant, Coach, Speaker (aka The Well Heeled Coach)

Shannon grew up within an entrepreneurial family, so began working from the age of five years in her grandmother's restaurant, and at 12 years old, she was doing the accounting and book keeping for various family businesses. After leaving school, Shannon moved into banking, and quickly moved up the levels to become the youngest officer they had in the bank. Shannon studied full-time at night while working full-time, and with this thirst for knowledge found herself quickly getting bored in the bank jobs she undertook. She would take on new roles, write the 'how to' manuals, and then move to the next role. During her maternity leave from the bank, Shannon worked part-time as an on-call officer, covering for management staff across the bank's state network. Through that exposure, Shannon's confidence and experience continued to develop such that after 20 years in banking she left to establish her own business. Shannon's business quickly moved from book keeping to working with businesses that were in transition or financial difficulty, where she reconstructed their financial statements. By doing that type of work, Shannon 'fell' into management consulting.

One of the biggest challenges Shannon faced was the decision to leave banking after 20 years; it was a comfortable career and the staff were like her extended family. After much deliberation, she left to set up a business where she found that the telephone did not ring and she did not have a pay cheque coming in each month. As an analytical, introverted personality type, Shannon found the idea of selling herself and her skill set to potential clients very intimidating. To manage and bypass this fear of sales, she relied heavily on her extensive network, developed during her long banking career. Shannon focused on re-establishing her credentials with the CPAs and banking lenders, and in return they referred business to her. As well, Shannon learnt the benefits of networking and using networks to build business relationships. Shannon now laughs at how she initially went six weeks without receiving a telephone call for business, then after a lot of networking, she received nine business opportunity telephone calls in one day! "Whew", she said!!

Since those early entrepreneurial days, Shannon's business has significantly grown and evolved. She is an advocate of lifelong learning, and continuously has coaches and mentors supporting her business success. When seeking a mentor, Shannon looks for someone who is in a field that she is in, with the same philosophy, but with more experience so she can learn from them. When seeking a business coach, Shannon looks for someone who is going to push her in areas she is not comfortable in, so that she is stretched to move beyond her own mental barriers, therefore achieving at a new level.

To be successful in business, Shannon believes: 1) You should not be afraid of failure. Very often people are so afraid that they over-analyse and paralyse themselves into inaction, such that nothing is accomplished. Shannon believes that failure is a valuable tool. 2) Make sure you have focus. Set goals and go for them but be clear on what the big picture for your business is, as it is easy to get distracted by new ideas. When a new idea arises, create and implement action steps in your business plan, even if they are small ones, so that you have forward momentum. 3) Talk about your goals so that others know what you want to achieve and can support you — whether those people be employees, family, coaches and mentors, or your network of business contacts and friends - put it out there. They will support you and hold you to account when you are checking in with them.

Adèle's Note: I really enjoyed interviewing Shannon. As it turns out we have similar backgrounds; trained accountants and former bankers turned consultants/business coaches. Given her personality type, perhaps one might think that Shannon is not a 'natural' entrepreneur, as they are often represented as highly outgoing/extroverted types. Shannon's success has put paid to that stereotype! By using her networks, Shannon has built a tremendously successful consulting practice, and has substantial business goals in place going forward. In particular, Shannon wants to support more women in becoming successful entrepreneurs, and with that success to create a Foundation where her successful women clients mentor and support young women in high schools and colleges to feel confident, understand their worth, and consider entrepreneurialism as a fantastic career option. A wonderful community based add-on to her business; a real example of 'giving back'.

To connect with Shannon Lea Reynolds:
W: www.shannonleareynolds.com
Tw: @WellHeeledCoach
FB: Shannon Lea Reynolds

Chapter 6

Cross, Up, Down And Frequently Selling

> Only those who risk going too far can possibly find out how far they can go. **T.S. Eliot**

In this chapter we are going to consider how you can offer your products and services so that your existing customers buy more each time they shop with you. We will also consider how you can encourage them to shop with you more often as selling more products and services to existing customers — as long as they are your most profitable products and services as we discovered in Chapter Four — is the easiest way to grow your business. It is much easier than continually finding new customers.

There are three key ways in which a business can increase its sales:

- Increasing the average order value (average transaction size) when an existing customer buys from the business.
- Increasing the average order frequency, meaning the existing customer buys from your business more often.
- Increasing the number of customers who buy from your business.

There are several techniques used to increase sales, including up-selling, down-selling, and cross-selling. Up-selling is getting customers to buy a more expensive product or service than they originally selected. A classic example is how for a dollar more McDonald's will supersize your order. Or, when buying a new car of any make, you are offered accessories to add to the enjoyment of the car, for instance, leather rather than vinyl/fabric upholstery.

Cross-selling is to offer products or services to the customer that in some way complements the item they are buying, such as when a waiter asks if you'd like a salad with your entrée. And down-selling is getting the customer to buy something, even if it means a lower priced item.

Up-Selling

Have you ever found yourself in a supermarket with your shopping list that you cross off as you shop, but then when you are at the checkout you realise that you have bought a lot more than you intended? That happens to just about everyone including me, especially when I am shopping with my daughter.

Supermarkets understand customer buying behaviour and they spend millions to ensure they get the customer experience right so that shoppers buy more. For instance, you might want to zip in to buy some bread, milk, and a newspaper. Have you noticed that you have to walk through most of the supermarket to buy those items? They are never placed together, even though they are fairly standard purchases, because the supermarkets know that if they space the milk, bread, and newspapers throughout the store, the customer is highly likely to purchase more goods as they shop.

Many of us shop for books or other goods on Amazon. When we select an item to buy, Amazon automatically has a page that says: customers who bought product X also bought product Y. Then they show us a selection of other products related to the one you have agreed to buy. Be honest: how often have you bought more books or other goods on Amazon, when you only intended to buy one thing? I do it all the time. I think I must be Amazon's best customer. Again, this is a perfect example of up-selling to customers.

So how can you use up-selling techniques in your business to sell more of your products or services? It is not a difficult exercise to achieve, it just requires thought.

In my experience, many businesses try to offer all their products and services as one offering, in a one-size-fits-all approach to their customers, whereas customers, whether they are individuals or companies, all have different needs and expectations. The key is to fully understand and separate out your products or services. Some examples:

- Offer your customer a more expensive product or service compared to the one they are currently considering. Once offered, the customer can then decide whether they want to invest in a lower-cost or higher-cost product. The key is to explain the features of the more expensive product very clearly to the customer, so they fully understand what they are getting for the increased money they spend.
- Offer your customer a more expensive brand. They may be considering a low end brand, but if you offer a higher end brand, explaining all its benefits, they may decide to opt for the upgrade.
- Offer warranties on products and services or, if you already have those as standard, offer extended warranties that are compelling to the customer.
- Offer three for two or five for three (multi-purchase) deals. These are very popular in the supermarket and lower end clothing industry. Once you have done your costings, you may find the marginal cost of giving away one or more product is much less than the sales price or gross margin of selling two or three products.
- Add an extra product to the offer, one that is cheaper buying through your business than if bought at another store. For instance, a florist may offer a box of chocolates or bottle of bubbly with a bouquet of flowers. If the customer perceives value in getting the box of chocolates or bubbly from you, they will add it to their order.

- Offer extra products to turn a standard product into a premium product. Ferrari car salespeople are masters at doing this. When a customer orders a Ferrari they are buying a basic model without frills, but they are offered a variety of extras from highly specified hubcaps and steering wheels to all sorts of other add-ons, so the customer feels compelled to buy them to get the Ferrari premium product.
- If you are in the services industry selling knowledge based products, you can sell basic, mid-range, and premium products to your customers by adding extra products or access to you at the premium end of your offering.

I love thinking about all the ways in which a business can up-sell its offering of products or services. In most businesses the opportunities are endless. What up-selling ideas can you create for your business?

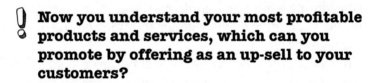

Now you understand your most profitable products and services, which can you promote by offering as an up-sell to your customers?

Cross-Selling

The key to successful cross-selling is to focus your efforts on meeting the customer's needs, rather than simply pushing any of your products and services. Many cross-selling opportunities happen organically. If you are selling pool cues, for example, you can also offer a bag, team shirts, shaping tools, and other accessories. Many hair salons also offer manicure services or massages. It is important, though, to stay relevant. Selling dog collars and pet toys at a hair salon isn't a natural extension for people getting their hair cut or coloured so it's likely to fail.

Other ways to facilitate cross-selling include:

- Recommendations. Some restaurants have the chef recommend a wine they feel would complement particular courses of the dinner.
- Training. It doesn't matter how great a strategy is if you cannot get your staff to enthusiastically and correctly implement it. Give your staff guidance on the best ways to incorporate cross-selling and up-selling.
- Utilise multi-platforms. Use your website and social media activity to inform customers of the variety of services and products your business offers. Consider special online deals: A salon could offer a buy one-get one free deal on selected shampoos when ordered online.
- Bundle. Offer a discount on a group of related items to entice shoppers to buy several related items.

Business is about creativity, and bundling products and services to meet customers desires and needs.

Down-Selling

Down-selling is used when your customer is thinking about not purchasing a product or service because it is outside their budget. Rather than losing the sale altogether, a smart sales person will offer the customer a cheaper option for the product or service they were looking to purchase, one that fits their budget.

While this is not a sales technique book, the key to success with this sales strategy is to wait until the very last moment, when you are certain the customer is not going to buy the more expensive product or service, then recommend a cheaper option, perhaps a less well known branded product. Make sure though that you let the customer know there is little difference between the two products.

For instance, when buying computers, well known brands are often substantially more expensive than lesser known brands, but essentially they do the same job. If the customer cannot afford the expensive brand, ensure as the sales person you have all the relevant knowledge in relation to the less expensive product, otherwise the customer will think you are doing a 'sales job' on them.

> **Down-selling is an opportunity to offer a customer a product or service that meets their budget. Never lose an opportunity to make a sale with a customer.**

Passion vs Apathy

You must have passion for your business so that the customer feels you are really authentic. Passion and apathy are obvious to spot and if a customer feels that you are apathetic they will not take up your offer.

For instance, in my local bookshop/stationers, they always offer chocolate for $1 at the sales counter. The checkout operator is told to make the offer and there is no passion in their voice. I am yet another number in their system so I always say no.

Yet, if the checkout operator said something like, "We have an amazing deal on this chocolate today. It's my personal favourite, because it is so creamy. Can I offer it to you today? I can promise it will put a smile on your face as you bite into it", being a sucker for a great sales pitch, I may well buy the chocolate simply because I was impressed with the presentation (I don't eat chocolate but my family loves it, so there will always be eager eaters).

> **Have you thought about whether your customers 'feel' your passion for your business when they talk to you and your staff?**

Product and Service Knowledge

To effectively up-sell your products or services, it is important that you have a full knowledge of them, including the benefits of the up-sold products that you are offering. If you do not and the customer discovers this when asking you questions they are going to feel that they are simply a number in your system and they may not be interested. Again, passion comes into play. On many occasions I am sure we have all bought something based on the passion of the salesperson rather than because we actually need a product or service. Certainly, I have.

> **Do you and your staff constantly update your product and service knowledge?**

Listen, Listen, and Observe

We have two ears, two eyes, and one mouth for a reason. At times it is very important to just observe our customers and listen to them. If your business is a shop, you can learn a lot by watching a customer. If a customer is uncertain about whether they will buy a product, often they will pick it up several times to look at it and to find out more about it. In that instance, you as the salesperson can talk to them about the benefits of the product. Similarly, listen to what they say they need. This is a golden opportunity to up-sell to a more highly specified or branded product if you explain the benefits of the product in relation to what the customer is saying they need.

> **Active listening and observing is a 'learned' skill, but done well, will result in increased sales.**

Accessorise, Accessorise, Accessorise

If a customer is very clear about the product they wish to purchase there is little to be gained from attempting to up-sell them to a more expensive product. Instead, focus on how you can up-sell extras that support the customer's choice of product.

For instance, my husband purchased a tablet computer. Having done his research, he was very clear on the brand he wanted so the salesperson did not attempt to up-sell him to another brand. Rather, the salesperson offered him a vast range of other products, including: a selection of trendy tablet covers to choose from at a reduced price; an antivirus package at a reduced price; 3G plug-ins to upgrade the tablet to be 3G accessible, and a variety of reduced priced apps to chose from. Very intelligent up-selling, if you ask me.

Remember the Ferrari story I told you earlier? How can you emulate that in your business? Think ahead for all the options you can give a customer related to the main product they have chosen to buy.

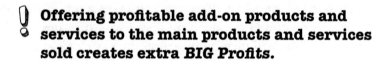 **Offering profitable add-on products and services to the main products and services sold creates extra BIG Profits.**

Partnering with Other Providers

This leads me to the possibility of giving away free products or services offered by joint venture partners to your business. If the customer accesses free products such as a free trial of something the joint venture partner offers, and then later purchases something from the joint venture partner, your business should be able to get a percentage of the sale.

You can also partner with other businesses, offering their services within your own, taking a profit margin along the way. Depending on the product or services you promote on behalf of the other business, your business will get a continuing fee or a one-off introducing fee from the business after your customer has become their customer. It depends on the nature of the product or service that you are promoting that is offered by another business. Regardless, it all adds to extra pure profit into your business.

There are so many opportunities to partner with complementary partners to your business. It just requires thinking about the logical product or service extensions you can offer that would be supplied by another business. Once you have determined suitable product and service extensions, then you would build a business relationship with the other provider, agreeing (in writing) the terms of the arrangement. Once done, then your business can make additional product and service offers to your customers, knowing that if they take up all or any of the offers, your business gets to 'clip the ticket' with additional gross income coming into your business. Classic examples of partnering include:

- When taking out a mortgage through a broker, being offered house insurance services through their insurance partner.
- Often (especially at the higher end of the real estate market) a realtor will offer to introduce their customers to an interior designer who could help the potential house buyer re-develop the house into the 'home of the new owner's dreams'.
- Online stores often offer for sale products they do not actually stock. They merely advertise and sell on behalf of another business, and the other business arranges delivery. John Lewis, a department store chain in the United Kingdom, are masters at this with their online shop, 'clipping the ticket' on the sales they make on behalf of other suppliers, as I discovered when I bought kitchen appliances from them.
- Printing businesses often do not make large format signs and banners, but by building a trusting relationship with businesses that do, the printer can be a 'one-stop-shop' for all the printing needs of a customer.

- Accountants that don't do book keeping can partner with a reliable book keeper to assist their customers, so that when the accountant receives 'the books' of the customer at year-end, they are in good order.
- Mechanics fix cars, but often don't do 'body-shop' repairs, so can build a relationship with a business that does that type of work, helping the mechanic's business to look like a 'one-stop-shop' for all car problems.

The list of partnering opportunities is endless. How can your business gain extra profit by partnering with appropriate joint venture partners to your business, thus also helping customers buy more from your business?

> **Partnering with other product and service providers provides a business with excellent additional gross income sources.**

Purchase Incentives

How many times have you bought more from a business when you have been told that if you order over X amount you will get free delivery, a free gift, or you are offered some other incentive? We all do it. That is called a purchasing incentive; enticing your buyer to buy more. How can you incentivise them to buy more?

Online businesses do this all the time. I constantly buy up to and beyond the free delivery amount as I feel I am getting better value from the online store. See how easily I get sucked into sales techniques even when I understand what the business is doing? Some well known examples include:

- Buy two and get the third item for free. Or, buy four and get the fifth item for free.
- Buy one and get the second item at half price.

- Buy products and services to a certain value and get a discount coupon for future purchases.
- Free delivery for purchases over a certain amount.
- Receive a free gift with purchases over a particular amount.
- Purchase certain products and services, and other complementary bundled products and services will also be given.

 Most businesses can create simple ways to offer purchase incentives to their customers. It takes thought and imagination, and a desire to stand apart from the competition, so that the business gets noticed and remembered.

Frequency of Purchase

As I mentioned at the start of the chapter, encouraging an existing customer to purchase from you more frequently is another key way to grow your business. Automation is a particularly valuable tool in encouraging your customers to buy more frequently.

As a consumer, how many emails do you receive a week making all sorts of offers of discounts and promotions on products and services? This is a key way in which businesses are driving more customers to their business in the modern digital world — by automatically keeping them updated on all the offers they have available at any one time.

Any business can automate more of its marketing activity. In order to do that, all your customer details must be placed into a simple database linked into auto responders that send out messages to them at certain times making offers and then providing easy ways for the customer to buy those offers. For instance, if you are an online business, then you would provide a link to the buying pages. If you are a shop, the messages would provide details of when the offers expire, urging the customer to visit their local store. If you are a services business, then the messages should provide a link for the customer to click on to connect to your business, letting you know they are interested and want you to make contact.

Databases and auto responders are not difficult to set up, but can feel scary when you are busy enough in your business already. Outsourcing this work to specialist providers is the best way in which to get the work done without occupying your time with it. Outsourced providers are the experts in the area and are not expensive to contract. It is their job to do this work for you, and the financial return is easily measurable; meaning the cost of the outsourcing partner should be far less than the sales revenue they bring to your business.

The opportunities to present offers about your business via email messages to your customers are endless, once you get the automated systems established.

In the United Kingdom, plumbers and gas engineers are far less busy in the summer months than in winter because when people turn on their central heating in winter, things often go wrong so there is a big demand for repairs. I am forever suggesting to plumbers and gas engineers that they make offers to service their customers' boilers and central heating systems during the summer months when they are less busy. If they automated presenting those offers to their customers, then the computer does all the work, once set up. Not only is it a passive way of effectively communicating with customers, where customers take up the offer, but it provides the plumbers and gas engineers with further sources of revenue to their business in summer and reduces the work pressure they always experience at the start of winter.

Automating offers to customers is one way in which a small business can encourage its customers to buy more frequently from it. Can your business benefit from automation to increase sales?

If your business doesn't want to approach customers in this way, then the traditional methods of advertising, leafleting, telephone-calling, and networking to present further compelling offers to customers will also hopefully result in them buying more frequently from your business, thereby improving your profitability.

 It is much harder finding new customers than it is to nurture and sell more to existing customers. Automating sales offers to customers is a passive and highly effective way to increase the purchasing frequency of customers to your business.

Personal Relationships with Customers

I wonder how many businesses have proactive meetings with customers to fully understand their needs and to educate customers about the products and services offered by their business. This is an excellent way of showing a customer that you really care about them and could well lead to further business with your existing customers. Now, if you are a shop owner this approach is not practical, but if you are a service provider this would be an excellent way of connecting with your customers to enhance the relationship and to win more business.

In my opinion, most customers to a business want to remain loyal to the business, but often it is the lack of feeling important that causes them to move away. So, if a customer is communicated with more often about their business and their needs, the chances are higher that they will remain loyal.

Hosting events to which customers are invited is also another way of building relationships with customers. The events don't have to be expensive, just appropriate to your business and to your customer. Similarly, meeting a customer over lunch or dinner helps them to feel important to your business, and therefore, loyal to you and your business.

> **Businesses that build personal relationships with customers enjoy significantly more loyalty and repeat business than those that do not.**

Loyalty Programmes

Loyalty programmes are an excellent way to encourage existing customers to buy more frequently from your business. It is estimated the number of loyalty programme members in the United States alone is two billion, with another 120 million members in Canada. The average United States household is actively participating in more than eight loyalty programmes. That should tell you something.

I quickly scanned the wallets of my husband and personal assistant, along with my own, to find that we had loyalty cards from the following types of businesses: coffee shops, book shops, pharmacies, clothing stores, soaps/cosmetics shops, chocolate shops, children's shoe shops, ice cream shops, bakeries, department stores, supermarkets, fitness boot camps, sandwich bars, sushi shops, and laundries. While most of the cards were for physical stores, for some businesses we accrue points via online sales too. Loyalty cards are not limited to stores. It just takes imagination in applying them to other types of businesses.

Loyalty cards don't have to give products away when a customer gets to a milestone. You can reduce the price of products upon the customer achieving a milestone. For instance, buy 10 and get the eleventh for half price. The point is, a little perceived appreciation can go a long way with customers, who are faced with tighter budgets and more options. By rewarding a customer for making a purchase, you can set your business apart; the first step towards securing a loyal customer. Research by Forrester Research found that loyalty programme members spend up to 13 percent more and loyalty programmes help drive return visits, meaning you can increase sales without having to drastically increase your customer base. Loyalty programmes can be a form of viral marketing because they can generate word of mouth business.

> **Many businesses can introduce some level of loyalty programme into their offering, to entice customers to buy more often over a certain period of time.**

Customer Experience Management

Bernd Schmitt, a professor of international business in the marketing department at Columbia Business School, is credited with coining the term 'customer experience management', or CEM, which he defines as "the process of strategically managing a customer's entire experience with a product or company".

The goal of CEM is to optimize the customer's experience to promote long-term customer loyalty, and its key aspect is that it looks at customer experience from the customer's perspective. The customer judges whether the experience was unacceptable or great. To that end, CEM is designed to understand and leverage the gap between current experience and desired experience from the customer's viewpoint in order to prevent future gaps.

In today's digital world, customer experiences are not relegated to traditional platforms such as purchases, customer service, or call centre communications, but are increasingly tied to social media. To manage the modern customer's experience, businesses need to establish a strategy that encompasses all customer touch points.

Bruce Temkin, Forrester Research vice president and principal analyst, believes the essence of CEM is treating customers as individuals. "Your customers don't live in spreadsheets; you need to go out and talk to them to understand who they are as people. That is, of course, unless each of your customers is really a 55 percent female with 2.3 kids who is 48 percent from a suburb and is 11 percent Hispanic."

The steps a business can use to improve customer experience include providing consistent customer experiences; giving customers a personalised experience; asking for customer feedback; acting on customer feedback; and measuring and analysing customer emotions through surveys, as mentioned previously. Generally speaking, customer feedback management programmes are supposed to enable businesses to peek inside the minds of customers. The information gleaned is used within the business to develop marketing plans, launch new products or services, and train staff.

Implementing CEM

Establishing a CEM strategy should be methodical so it integrates organically with your business. The first step is to identify any problem area that might be causing a loss of customers and rectify the situation. For example, if customers have to wait around to ask a question because they can't find a salesperson, perhaps it's time to hire more employees. Or if customers are unable to easily locate items, consider reorganizing your store – your physical or online store, as the point is relevant to both.

One of my greatest bugbears are small businesses that only use mobile phones, and when a customer calls, there is no answer phone to enable a message to be left, or a lack of professionalism in the telephone answering techniques of the business owner or employee. Nothing can be quicker in losing a business opportunity than an inappropriate telephone manner. Again, if customers were given the opportunity to provide feedback to the small business, perhaps the business owner would consider employing a telephone answering service to enhance the professionalism of their business.

Next, determine which touch points matter most to your customer base and work to improve those experiences. It's not necessary to try and concentrate on every touch point, just those that appear to matter the most to your customers.

Lastly, think outside the box for ways to innovate your customer's experience. Something as simple as a refreshment corner with complimentary coffee, soft drinks, and cookies will make customers feel more special and cared for. Or offer special deals through social media. Or send a greeting card to say thank you after you have finished doing a job for a customer. Very often, it is the small things that make a lasting impression.

Throughout the process, remember that CEM is just one part of a customer's total value proposition in relation to buying from your business. In other words, as important as experiences are, products, price and other aspects also matter. Make sure that your website, social media, customer service, staff and/or sales staff are complementary.

> **As the saying goes, doing 10 things 10 percent better than the competition is more effective than doing one thing 100 percent better.**

Pushing the Customer's Buttons

The idea behind commerce is simple: people pay a business money to buy a product or service they need. Those basic transactions are very straightforward, but what about all the things people buy that they don't need, from a new pair of designer shoes on sale to a facial when they go in for a haircut?

According to consumer behaviourist Barry Feig, author of *Hot Button Marketing*, most people don't buy out of need. "They buy on an emotional response then justify the purchase *after* they buy."

Fieg explains, "A hot button is an emotional pull; it is a turn-on for the consumer. It's how you talk about your product and speak directly to a consumer's needs in terms of his or her personal buying motivations."

Rather than trying to change what consumers think or feel about a product, it's much more effective to work within a consumer's mindset. While a book could be written on this topic alone, the key to establishing relationships with your customers is to understand their hot buttons, so that you can effectively market your products and services to them (pressing their hot buttons) to encourage a sale. Regardless of what your business offers, your customers will rely more on emotion for determining purchases than logic or need. Since our basic physical needs are fulfilled, you need to engage your customer's wants. Wants create new needs, which mean more sales and bigger profits.

The most common hot buttons include a desire for status; the excitement of discovering something new or unique; revaluing, which is a return to products used at an earlier time of their lives; family values; camaraderie; having fun or getting enjoyment; time management; achieving superlatives — the best of whatever; achieving dreams; lust; caring for others' well-being; reinvention; self-improvement; the desire to be powerful or influential; and dream fulfilment.

The point to remember is that modern society provides for most of our physical needs so it is our emotional and psychological needs that are more often than not unmet. By focusing on and selling to those needs, you can both improve your bottom line and establish deep customer loyalty.

Identifying the 'hot buttons' of a customer and focusing on them with sales offerings will result in increased sales which leads to increased profits.

Adèle McLay, the Agitator
There you have it. All you need to know about how to sell more to your existing customers. Ideally, before making up-selling, cross-selling or down-selling offers to your customers, your business will know which of your products and services are most profitable, so that you can use those products and services as the lever to entice your customers, and if they buy more, your business enjoys bigger profits.

 Strategy 9

Sell More to Your Current Customers to Increase your Business Profitability

Up-selling, cross-selling and down-selling your most profitable products and services to existing customers is the quickest way to increase business profits. Most businesses have a myriad of ways in which they can segment their customer market and product and service offering to entice customers to buy more. One size does not fit all. Product and service knowledge, listening to and observing customers, and actually being interested in your customers is critically important to increasing sales.

Customer experience management is also important, so that your customers return to your business time and time again in view of the value proposition your business offers them.

Finally, increasing the frequency with which customers buy from a business increases profits. Automation of offers is the most effective way in which to achieve increased purchases by customers.

Phil Turner

Electrician and until recently owner of a Fujitsu Heat Pump Franchise

I have known Phil Turner as the electrician for my property investment business in New Zealand for over 10 years. He and his team have always been excellent providers of service as electricians, totally focused on giving great customer service at fair prices. On the back of that, Phil built up a successful electrical contracting business.

While on holiday in 2007, Phil learnt about the international heat pump industry; at the time, The Netherlands was predicted to be the next big market for the industry. Phil returned to New Zealand, did his research, and decided to purchase a heat pump franchise through Fujitsu. Because most New Zealand homes are not centrally heated, the heat pumps are used in New Zealand to warm houses in winter and cool them in summer; the technology was moderately new to the country at the time. Phil had always wanted to own a product focused rather than service business, and felt that the heat pump industry was a natural progression from being an electrician, so took on the new business and industry with a business partner, Gareth.

Fujitsu New Zealand was impressed with Phil's business plan, so embraced the new business supporting them with advertising investment. When they started, Phil and Gareth had budgeted to install four heat pumps per week; in fact, at times they were installing six per day and had a four week waiting list. Phil notes that they could have installed 10 units a day if they had had the staff to support them.

Initially Phil and Gareth used a home delivered magazine to advertise in, but eventually focused their marketing and advertising budget on Google AdWords, as it was the means by which they received most of their customer leads. Phil's wife is an accountant, so supported the business with day to day accounting and administration.

Phil notes the business's greatest achievement was being Fujitsu's number one dealer in the country; something they achieved after two years, to the delight of Fujitsu, Phil and Gareth.

The industry got very competitive as more heat pump companies entered the market. And, as often happens when a new market matures, Phil's business ended up competing with one-man-bands who operated out of home without the business overheads.

After five incredibly successful years, in 2013 Phil and Gareth decided to sell the business after being made an offer they couldn't refuse. At the time of the interview, Phil was still coming to terms with not being in the business, noting he had just booked his first decent holiday in five years.

After taking a good holiday, and in light of enjoying the experience of selling a product, Phil is considering other product ideas that draw on his electrical contracting experiences. He is too young to retire, and besides, he loves the cut and thrust of being in business.

Adele's Notes: Phil and Gareth were really pleased with the way in which they ran their very successful business. If they had continued in it, in view of competition, they would have to have reviewed their business overheads in order to increase profits, but at the time they achieved the financial success they were seeking. Phil and Gareth should be an inspiration to anyone seeking to break out of a business they know into something new. If you apply your business knowledge to the new industry and are passionate about achieving success, you will do it. Then the rewards are there for reaping – great profits; selling out for an excellent price; lifestyle.

Chapter 7

Pricing: The Scariest Part Of Business?

> Price is only an issue when value is not perceived.
> **Phil Berg**

The price you establish for the sale of your products and services in your business is arguably one of the most important business decisions you will make. And yet, pricing is one of the most feared elements in managing a business.

One of the main conversations I have with business owners is on pricing, and those discussions usually start with me saying, "Your prices are too low." They look at me in shock and generally respond with all the reasons why they cannot raise their prices:

- I've lost jobs because I was too expensive.
- I'm more expensive than some of my competitors.
- I'm barely making enough profit as it is, and I can't afford to lose customers by raising prices.
- You have got to be joking — put my prices up in this depressed market?

Responses like that generally indicate those business owners don't understand the impact pricing has on a customer's perception of their business and its branding in the market. It also means the business owner is a victim of their business rather than the master or mistress of it.

If your prices are too low, your market will label you a low-end player and you'll attract bargain hunters who will invariably try to get you to discount your products even further. Lower prices also make it unlikely your business will build long-term relationships with customers, who by their very nature will shop around to get the best prices on a product or service, not staying loyal to any one business.

Higher pricing raises customers' expectations of a business, which can be a challenge. But if you constantly deliver on those expectations your business will usually enjoy customer loyalty, and you will attract a better quality customer that is willing to pay more for quality customer service.

This book is all about helping your business make *BIG Profits*. Remember, there are only two ways in which a business can grow its profit:

- Increasing sales.
- Reducing expenses.

Let's take a look at the impact a price increase could have on the profitability of a business. For this simple exercise, XYZ Limited has 200 customers. The average value of a sale is $1,000 and the cost of goods sold for each product is $300. The business's fixed costs are $90,000 per annum. Table 7a demonstrates the impact of XYZ increasing its prices by 2 percent, 5 percent, and 10 percent.

	Current $	Increase $	Increase $	Increase $
Gross Sales	200,000	204,000	210,000	220,000
Less Cost of Goods Sold	-60,000	-60,000	-60,000	-60,000
Gross Profit	140,000	144,000	150,000	160,000
Less Expenses	-90,000	-90,000	-90,000	-90,000
Net Profit Before Tax	50,000	54,000	60,000	70,000

Table 7a: XYZ Limited – Impact of Price Increases

In this example, when there is a 2 percent price increase, the business profit increases by $4,000 per annum or 8 percent in one year. With a 5 percent price increase, the profit increases by $10,000 or a 20 percent increase. With a 10 percent price increase, the profit of the business increases by a whopping $20,000 or 40 percent.

With all things being equal, increasing your prices by a small amount results in a compounding increase in profit.

It is important to note that increasing prices has no impact on cost of goods sold, which is based on quantity of products sold not the sales price.

When considering raising your prices, ask yourself, "If I do increase my prices, will I be the most expensive business in my industry?"

Your answer is highly likely to be no. If the answer is yes, then you are at the premium end of your industry serving the most discerning customers, and therefore price is unlikely to be the most important factor in their decision making process. Even if you are at the premium end of the market, there is a strong argument that you should still raise your prices, making sure your customer service remains second to none, as it is the value proposition your business offers your customers that they will be most interested in.

My approach to pricing is: charge what you and your business are worth. Don't undersell yourself.

Let's use the example of a successful mobile car body repair business. I will call the owner Mike. His customers like his team arriving at their home or office to repair dings and dents on their motor vehicles. Mike's value proposition to his customers is:

- Repairs will be done within 48 hours.
- Repairs will be done at the location of the customer's choice for their convenience.
- All work is guaranteed.

Mike has a number of contractors who do the work on the customer's vehicles. Whether the work is a one-off repair or fleet repairs, Mike is highly visible to his customers, and they love his hands-on, very caring, customer-centric approach. Nothing is too much trouble for Mike and his team. As a result, he can charge a premium price for his services. His pricing is not the cheapest or the most expensive in the local market, but Mike charges his customers for the value his business offers and in turn Mike's customers have never questioned the cost of the work.

Even so, I would have still challenged him to consider the positive impact on his business by raising his prices by 5 or 10 percent.

In another example, Peter sells and installs carpets. He too is very hands-on and has a small installation team that works with him. He works with a range of customers in the residential and commercial market.

Peter and his team are loved by all his customers and most of his work comes by repeat business and referrals. His pricing is not the most expensive in the industry, and he and his team are hugely respected. Peter's company does a lot of work for elderly customers, and he says that one of the reasons he gets so much work in that market is that he doesn't charge extra for moving all the customer's furniture and possessions when laying the carpet. I have challenged Peter to raise his prices by around $50 per order and to list on his invoices all the work his business does for his customers at no extra charge.

So far he has not taken my advice even though he knows he will make extra profit every year if he did. Nor does he break down his services on the invoice to show what is charged for and what is free. I am certain that if Peter did break down his invoices to show the chargeable products and services from the services delivered for free, his customers would appreciate Peter and his team even more, and would not notice an extra $50 per order.

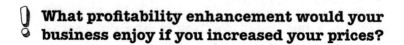

What profitability enhancement would your business enjoy if you increased your prices?

Let's explore the concern that if you raise prices, you will lose too many customers.

Using my earlier example, let's assume that XYZ increased its prices by 10 percent, and that had a corresponding impact of losing 20 percent of its customers. That means its customer base would drop from 200 to 160; the average value of a sale would increase to $1,100; COGS would remain at $300 per sale. Look at the impact of this change to the business in Table 7b.

	Original Pricing $	10% Sales Increase 20% Drop in Customers $
Gross Sales	200,000	176,000
Less Cost of Goods Sold	-60,000	-48,000
Gross Profit	140,000	128,000
Less Expenses	-90,000	-90,000
Net Profit Before Tax	50,000	38,000

Table 7b: XYZ Limited – Financial Impact of Losing 20% of Customers

Using this example, the business does lose $12,000 in profit when it increases its prices. But let me point out that it is highly unlikely that you will lose 20 percent of your customers by raising your prices by a small amount; they will generally leave for reasons other than price.

Let me remind you of the *L4 Customer Profitability Quadrant* we explored in Chapter Five. Remember the bottom left quadrant, titled '*Lose Them*'? The customers most likely to leave your business if you raise prices are the ones who are not loyal to your business anyway. They are highly price driven. So, would it matter if you lost them, given your enjoyment factor of them is low? Don't you want to lose them anyway?

Think again about the types of customers you want your business to attract. They are in the top right *'Lots More'* quadrant. Those customers are unlikely to leave your business due to a price rise, as they value the customer service proposition you offer and pricing is often the least of their concerns.

Losing customers in the *'Lose Them'* quadrant gives you more time to focus on getting more of the *'Lots More'* customers and moving some of your *'Look Out'* and many of your *'Lift Up'* customers into the *'Lots More'* quadrant.

Let's think more about the impact of losing customers. Using this example, if you increased your price by 10 percent and lost 20 percent of your customers, that is suggesting one in every five customers would leave your business. As the business owner, if you did nothing to address this by finding more customers in the *'Lots More'* quadrant you want to attract, then there is likely to be an impact on your business overhead in that you would be able to reduce some of your fixed costs.

However, given you will have more free time in your business as you are not servicing the 20 percent of customers who left and who were time consuming anyway, how about using that newly found time to market your business to the types of customers you do want?

Dr Michael LeBoeuf, international business consultant, focuses a lot of his work on how to win customers and keep them. He created a matrix based on extensive research on why customers leave a business.

Reasons Why Customers Leave

Perceived Indifference	68%
Unresolved Conflict	14%
Get a Better Deal/Pricing	9%
Influenced Away	5%
Move Away	3%
Die/Insolvent	1%

Table 7c: Reasons Why Customers Leave

Table 7c demonstrates that, based on that research only 9 percent of customers leave due to pricing, whereas 82 percent of customers leave because they are not treated as special or there is an unresolved conflict. In essence, they leave due to a lack of customer service.

If you are still not convinced, HelpScout, an American software company, using a range of research data sources from reputable Fortune 500 companies, determined that 86 percent of consumers "quit doing business with a company because of a bad customer experience".

Therefore, key to the success of your business is not worrying about price increases you may want to introduce, but concentrating on the customer service proposition you deliver to your customers to keep them happy and returning for more.

> **How brave are you feeling about increasing your prices? Remember, customers don't usually leave due to price increases. They leave due to lack of customer service.**

Cost vs Price vs Value in Pricing

The terms cost, price, and value are often used when discussing pricing, so it is important to clarify what they really mean.

- **Cost:** the amount you spend to buy or manufacture your product or services (cost of goods sold or COGS).
- **Price:** the amount you charge your customers for providing the product or service.
- **Value:** what your customer believes your product or service is worth to them.

Consider a situation where a homeowner arrives home to find all the electricity is out; the food in the refrigerator is going bad; there's no hot water for bathing; and no electricity to cook a meal. So the local electrician is telephoned for an emergency service.

The cost of the materials and travelling expenses to fix the problem might be $50, and an hour's labour to pay the electrician might be $25 per hour, plus profit margin of, say, $25. Therefore the cost to the customer could be $100. However, the business owner electrician will price their services on their ability to quickly identify the problem based on their qualifications and experience so the customer is minimally disrupted. The customer is likely to value the benefit of having the problem solved quickly so they can get on with their life. By understanding this market, the electrician might be able to price the job at $120 or more, therefore making an extra profit of $20 or more.

Let's look at an example of an interior designer, who creates magnificent homes for her customers to live in. Typically, interior designers charge an hourly rate or project rate for their work, plus they will add a margin onto the products they buy for the customer such as fabric for curtains, furnishings and furniture. If the interior designer is working with customers in the middle income bracket where hiring an interior designer is a luxury, then they will have to carefully select their hourly rate and margin because there is possibly a lot of competition by other interior designers for work at that level in the customer market. A good interior designer will hopefully price at the high end of what that market can bear, by evidencing the value their customers will get by working with them according to their needs.

If the interior designer is working at the luxury end of the interior design market where the customers have very deep pockets, they are making their selection of interior designer not based on price but on the skills and experience the interior designer brings to the project to create the home the customers have dreamed about. Therefore, the interior designer can price their work extremely highly based on the value they offer to their customers at the premium end of that market. If the interior designer was to price their work too cheaply with these customers, chances are they wouldn't get the job because the customer would perceive the interior designer to be less skilled or able to deliver the quality of home they are looking for.

So, key to setting out your pricing strategy is to determine:

- The market in which you are competing.
- The factors which are important to your customers as they make their buying decisions.
- The benefits you are offering to your customers in relation to their buying decisions.
- The value customers place on your product or service.

Pricing is not an arbitrary decision; all businesses should have a pricing strategy. When determining your business's pricing strategy, the key is to determine your value proposition for your customers, rather than pitching your business against your competition and attempting to undercut them to win more customers.

> **Businesses that have a pricing strategy and stick to it, and are clear about the value proposition they offer their customers enjoy much higher profits than those that do not.**

Quoting and Following Up

I cannot believe how many businesses spend vast amounts of time preparing quotes for their potential customers, send off the quote via email or mail, and then wait.... and wait.... and wait. That behaviour is *ridiculous*. Spending all the effort on a quote then doing nothing sends out the wrong messages.

But first, let's get back to basics in relation to quoting for a piece of work.

What happens when you get an opportunity to quote for a piece of work? Do you and/or your sales staff take down the requirements of the potential customer; make a couple of recommendations as appropriate; prepare a quote, which you send off to your customer? That is what most businesses do, and as a result they miss out on a number of marketing, customer service and potential sales opportunities.

While this book is not a 'how to be effective in sales and negotiation' book per se, if done correctly, more business can be won by small businesses if they approach the quoting process more effectively. More sales, if priced correctly, leads to a more profitable business.

The first lesson in effective quoting is to *qualify* your potential customer. That means you, the business owner, asks lots of questions of the potential customer to really understand what they are wishing to buy. With suitable questioning, you can identify their *hot buttons*; qualify their price point requirements (if they have any), customer service expectations, delivery timeline expectations, and a lot more. In essence, by asking questions of your potential customer before you even think about writing a quote for them, you can get all the answers you need in order to write a winning quote. After qualifying the potential customer, you can prepare a quote that directly provides for all the requirements they have, so the potential customer is compelled to accept your quote, as you have offered them everything they say they are wanting.

Through effective questioning, you can also determine if you actually *want* to quote for the work. For instance, you might find that a potential customer is so price sensitive, they are shopping around to get the cheapest quote. If your business is a premium branded business, you do not want to diminish your brand by price slashing to win business. By understanding your potential customer's requirements, you can then decline to quote as you will not be able to effectively service them. Those types of customers are likely to fall into the *'Lose Them'* quadrant of your *L⁴ Customer Profitability Quadrant,* and you don't want any more of those. So don't quote for them in the first place.

When a quote is prepared for a potential customer, I firmly believe that whenever possible, a quote should be personally delivered, whether face-to-face or by Skype. Talking a potential customer through your quote, using the language they used, and addressing all the points that were of interest or concern to them when you were qualifying them, should, if done effectively, result in your business winning the sale. Why? Because your quote should have satisfied all their needs and *hot buttons*, providing a win/win for both parties.

Finally, if you have addressed all the buying decision factors in your quote so that the potential customer is happy, then don't be afraid to *ask for the sale.*

This is another of my bugbears: too many businesses are afraid to let the potential customer know that they want to work with them. Let your potential customer know that you would be delighted to work with them. Make them feel very special to your business.

> **Quoting for new business often takes a considerable amount of time, so no business can afford to waste time quoting for work that is not suited to them. Once a quote is given, don't be afraid to follow up.**

Brand Perception

There are many factors that combine to form a person's identity. The same is true with a business. Generally speaking, your business's identity is how it is presented to customers; its persona. A properly crafted identity presents its message consistently, which in turn is essential in developing your business's brand. Research has found that companies with a consistent identity are taken significantly more seriously than companies without. That translates into bigger profits.

A common mistake is to confuse company identity with company image. The two concepts are related but there are important distinctions. While your business identity is about how you want your business to look to customers, image is how the customers actually perceive the business.

Ideally, a business's identity and image are synchronised. For example, Apple's identity is that of a forward thinking high-tech company; its image is one of innovation. That synergy has helped Apple become one of the most profitable companies in the world.

Marketing coach Kathy Ellis says a customer's relationship with a business has an important visceral component. "When your identity and image match, you've created a bond, a trust, with your customer. This then becomes your compelling, differentiating value proposition."

Building relationships with customers is an ongoing process; it's not a one-and-done occurrence. It requires a personal investment. But in order to develop and maintain these relationships, you need to have a clear understanding about what business you're really in; what you are truly promising your customers.

Consumer behaviourist Barry Feig explains this concept with a story about Kodak founder George Eastman, who once asked his sales team what product they were selling. One person said cameras, another said pictures, and a third said film. Eastman shook his head and explained that all those answers were side-products. What they were really selling was memories. Similarly, it can be argued that McDonald's became a global empire by selling convenience.

Among the benefits you can expect from establishing a strong brand are:

- Customers can quickly and easily identify your business in a variety of marketing platforms.
- Your business will project professionalism.
- Your company will become more easily remembered than your competitors.
- Prospective customers will understand what your business does.
- Customers will have confidence buying your product.
- Other companies may want to collaborate with you.

Some of these benefits will be almost immediate; others will come over time.

Brand perception is an important factor in pricing. If your brand identity and image in the eyes of your customers is that of a premium brand, you will be able to charge much higher prices than if your brand perception is at the other end of the market.

 Branding is invaluable to a business and its importance is often ignored by small business owners.

Premium Pricing Follows Premium Branding

After your business is perceived as a premium brand, you can implement premium pricing. Most people look for ways to save money so the key is convincing them they are getting better overall value even though they are paying a premium. You must explain to customers why your prices are higher and how it benefits them.

Don't just talk the talk. You must also walk the walk. And that starts with your sales people and all staff. It's a given that they should be friendly and polite but they also need to anticipate your customers' needs, wants, and desires. Premium pricing means providing premium customer experience from start to finish.

Do not dilute your premium pricing, even if going through a slow period. Paul Spiegelman, author of *Why is Everyone Smiling? The Secret behind Passion, Productivity, and Profit,* says, "Another disadvantage to playing the discount game is that this strategy is the fastest way to push your product or service into the commodity category. Select businesses have carved out a distinctive market by not discounting their products. The challenge is to create and sustain a brand that supports your premium pricing strategy."

> **Premium pricing is the way to BIG Profits, only if the total customer experience is consistent with the premium brand you are offering. If the value received is less than desired, the premium branding will not be effective, and premium pricing will not be accepted in the future.**

Tiered and Bundled Pricing

One way to accommodate both premium customers and those on more of a budget is to offer tiered or bundled services or products.

Tiered pricing is when a business offers customers a variety of price points. One of the best known examples is car dealerships. Potential customers are first shown the base model. Then they are given the option for extras that range from a better radio to a fully loaded car. The lesson is that products presented at multiple price points can offer a larger number of potential buyers the incentive to buy something from your business.

Other benefits of tiered pricing include:

- **Consumer converts**. Offering a lower value item can give a customer the incentive to try a new product or service. For example, they may try a 20 minute massage and love it so much that the next time they buy a 60 minute session.
- **Reputation**. Tiered pricing enables new customers to sample your product or service. A good experience helps the business build a reputation and will give customers the confidence to try more expensive services.
- **Expand your customer base**. Offering different price points means you can accommodate customers with varying budgets.

Price bundling is a separate strategy where a seller bundles several different goods or services and sells it for a discounted price when compared to the value of each individual item. Telecom and cable companies have made millions using this strategy and it works just as efficiently for smaller business. For example, a salon may bundle a haircut, color, and blow dry for $100, when services may cost $45, $55, and $15 individually. The customer feels they have gotten a discount and good value for their money and the salon sold extra services.

Whatever strategies you employ, just remember that pricing is a primary determinant of a business's financial success because prices don't only determine gross income, they also impact a customer's perception of your business. Picking the right price points can be the difference between reliable cash flow and profits (but hopefully *BIG Profits*) and financial instability.

> **Consider your pricing decisions carefully
> — your business depends on it.**

Adèle McLay, the Agitator

In my experience, many businesses undervalue the products and services they offer their customers. When I started my consulting business, there was a lot of competition in the market. The first thing I worked on was our company's value proposition to our potential clients. Once that was defined, I then set our prices higher than most of our competitors, knowing that we as a business had to deliver more and better to justify our increased prices. We did and the business thrived.

What is the value proposition your business offers its customers? Do you have an appropriate pricing structure in place to support that value proposition? I hope so. If not, perhaps it is time you thought about this with your business adviser.

Strategy 10

Pricing for Big Profits and Business Success

Branding and a clear understanding of the value proposition a business offers its customers should drive pricing decisions. A premium brand should never under-sell its products and services as that behaviour diminishes the value of the brand. Similarly, a low-end brand cannot over-price its products and services.

By having a clear understanding of the business's brand values and delivering to its value proposition, often pricing is not an issue with customers, therefore a small business can increase its prices and not lose its quality or 'Lots More' customers.

Customers who do leave when prices are increased are most often the 'Lose Them' and 'Look Out' customers, who are a risk to a small business anyway.

Phil Berg

Former Carpet Business Owner, Now a Motivational Speaker, Sales Trainer and BNI Assistant National Director UK & Ireland and Regional Franchise Owner

While hoping to 'make it' as a footballer in the United Kingdom, Phil worked part-time for a family owned carpet shop in his local village. After determining that football was not to be his career, Phil worked full time in the carpet business. Later he had the opportunity to establish his own business in the same industry, and over 32 years he built the business up, selling it in 2007.

Early on in his career, Phil realised that to be successful in business one had to be perceived as being better than, and remembered by customers ahead of, the competition. Being naturally competitive, Phil sought out those in his industry who had many years experience already and whom he respected, and asked to be unofficially mentored. Most were responsive, so according to Phil, he was able to 'pick the brains' of others as they were always willing to help him. Through this mentoring, Phil learnt a lot, which he applied to his business and achieved considerable success.

One of Phil's key beliefs is that for a customer, price is never an issue – but value is! His business focused on giving exceptional value to his customers at all times. It wasn't doing one or two things 100 percent better than any other carpeting business, it was doing lots of elements of the business better than others. As well, he quickly realised that to grow a business, new potential customers had to 'meet the business', so through networking he developed the skills to promote his business to the target markets he was seeking to draw into his business. For instance, he built strong relationships with 'introducers' – people who work with people who may be able to introduce his business, including: interior designers, builders, property developers. Those individuals referred his business to their contacts, as they respected Phil and the work he and his staff did.

Phil believes it is better to be the one remembered first than to be the one who's best. The more friends you have, the more people say: "Go and use them. They are very good." Phil's business success was built on reputation.

Since selling his carpet business, Phil has become more involved with the international networking and referral organisation, BNI (Business Network International). In that capacity, Phil travels the world coaching BNI members on how to get the most out of their BNI membership and how to grow their business by referral marketing. Phil has also developed a sales coaching business where he coaches and gives keynote speeches on sales training and networking.

To be successful in business, Phil believes a business owner must: 1) Set challenging goals. 2) Set a date by which you want to achieve those goals. 3) Plan and constantly review progress towards those goals. 4) Believe in yourself, even when people try to put you off along the way.

Adèle's Note: Phil is an inspiration. From very humble beginnings he developed a hugely successful multi-site business, which he sold in 2007 just before the market crashed – timing is everything. Since then, he has gone on to re-invent himself and travels the world coaching others towards their own business success. While he acknowledges that he may not have the work/life balance quite right at times, Phil has a lovely family life, being married to Jacqui – his first and only true love - and together they have two children. Phil believes he is blessed to have a great family life, lots of friends in his world, and a successful career.

To connect with Phil Berg:
W: www.reachyourgoals.co.uk
Tw: @philberg88

Entrepreneur Profile

Chapter 8

Finding '*Lots More*' Customers!

> Whenever you see a successful business, someone once made a courageous decision.   **Peter Drucker**

I often hear how hard it is getting new customers. I don't disagree. New customer development can be a challenge to any business, but with a planned approach, a process can be applied, and more success can be guaranteed.

Creating a Customer Profile to Maximise Market Share

No business can be everything to all consumers. But you can maximise your market share by focusing on the type of customer you serve best. Once you have a basic idea of who your customer is, there are a number of ways to use that information to develop appropriate marketing plans and strategies.

Segmentation

If your goal is to reach a mass market, different segments of consumers will require different marketing approaches because one size does not fit all. You can break down your potential customer base into segments based on any number of parameters, such as geographic location, consumer behavior, or product usage.

Positioning

Positioning includes all efforts to establish your product, services and business in customers' minds. Once you do that, to stay top of mind will require continual vigilance because competitors will always be looking to get into your customer's head.

Targeting

Once segmented, decide how many consumer segments you can realistically afford to target and then create a separate marketing strategy for each.

Niche vs Differentiation

The most extreme targeting is niche marketing because it focuses on one narrow demographic. For example, suppose there are two bicycle stores. One offers a variety of bikes: children's, touring, road, two-seaters, and mountain bikes. But the other decides to go after the niche mountain bike market. The upside for them is they can concentrate their full marketing weight on this segment. The downside is they ignore a big chunk of general bike consumers. However, for certain businesses the trade-off is worth it.

In *Marketing Times,* C. Gail Tibbo explains, "Most business relationships work on the 80/20 rule: 80 percent of your revenue (and more likely 80 percent of your profits) come from 20 percent of your customers. Those who fit into this lucrative 20 percent deserve most of your attention — imagine how much effort is expended marketing to the 80 percent of customers who generate only 20 percent of profits. Simply, this fact makes a solid case for niche markets."

She also notes, "A strong position that targets a market niche is much more likely to help you make a dent in the market. It provides your business with an identity, and gives customers who are unfamiliar with your business a reason to consider dealing with you."

In differentiated marketing, a product or service is aimed at two or more specific segments. So the first bike store decides to target several segments — children and pleasure riders — which may very well include adults who want to ride with their young kids — and develops specific marketing strategies aimed at each group. Ideally, this strategy builds greater loyalty and repeat business by considering the needs and wants of a wider group of consumers. The downside is there are often higher marketing costs.

For a business to thrive there must be an active, ongoing marketing strategy to attract the ideal customer. Managing that process requires detailed information about your products or services, your potential and current customers, and a strategy that employs anything from promotional giveaways to community sponsorships. Marketing needs to be active in both the digital and analogue worlds to reach its full potential.

 Clarity over a business's target market is key!

Using the *L⁴ Customer Profitability Quadrant*

We previously explored the *L⁴ Customer Profitability Quadrant*. We found in the top right quadrant the customers most profitable to your business and the most enjoyable to work with. If you are targeting business to business (B2B) customers, for each customer in the *'Lots More'* Quadrant:

- What industry are they in?
- What size of business are they in their industry?
- What is your business's 'value' proposition to that business?

If you are targeting business to consumer customers:

- What are their demographics?
- What are their geographics?
- What are their psychographics?
- What are their ethnographics?
- What are their behavioural patterns?

Depending on the nature of your business, you may or may not be able to easily answer the above questions yourself. It not, then there are many ways in which you can glean the information, from contracting specialist market research companies to creating your own survey which can be sent to your customers on email via the various free online survey tools that are widely available.

Once you have information on the profiles of your best current customers, doesn't it make sense to seek out more of the same types of customers? While you won't be able to ascribe an *'enjoyment'* factor for the potential customers, there may well be common characteristics within your *'Lots More'* quadrant that enables you to make an initial assumption that the enjoyment factor may be strong. For instance, if you are very successful at servicing the hairdressing industry, with those types of customers being your most enjoyable and profitable customers, perhaps you should be targeting more hairdressing customers rather than finding customers in industries that you have not worked with before.

Tools for Seeking Out New Customers

From email marketing to social media to direct mail to promotional giveaways and traditional advertising, to networking and sponsorships, there are a wide variety of tools and strategies available to market a business. The skill is in determining the options that work best to target the most likely customers for your particular products or services. There is also a difference between the marketing you might do to generate new customers and marketing to keep your brand uppermost in your customers' minds to increase the odds they will refer you to others.

Here are some of the most effective strategies for attracting new customers and keeping current ones.

Flyers and Brochures
In the current digital-fueled world, flyers might seem quaint. But this admittedly analogue tool remains very effective because it

enables you to target your audience, especially within a confined geographic location. Suppose you own a pet store and are having a special sale. You can ask local vets, kennels, and groomers to keep a stack of flyers on their counters because customers of those businesses are people interested in pet supplies.

The key to an effective flyer is for it to be eye-catching without being too busy. You don't want the design elements to overshadow or bury your message. Spend the money on good paper because it reflects professionalism and quality. Try to find a printer that uses soy inks. Besides being environmentally friendly, the colors are crisp and vibrant, and are economical as well.

Be careful not to clutter the flyer with too much information. You want the potential customer to be able to see the message immediately. One 'eye-catcher' is to have the flyer double as a coupon. Offering a 10 or 20 percent discount on a specified transaction when the flyer is presented is a way to get people to at least glance over the flyer.

A brochure is like the flyer's more sophisticated cousin. It's designed to hold more information and presents a very polished image, if done correctly. Graphics and images are an important aspect of a brochure but too much will make it harder for the reader to zero in on the message or information being imparted. The copy used on a brochure should stay on topic and concentrate on the product or service being promoted because potential customers want to know how they will benefit. Because of their relative sturdiness and information density, brochures are frequently used for bulk-mailing campaigns.

Gift Certificates

Handing out gift certificates is a proven strategy to bring in more new customers. I've seen some businesses double the number of new customers, but on average you can expect at least a 5-10 percent increase.

Like any marketing strategy, gift certificates will not work if you don't work them — simply placing them on the counter will not automatically bring in new customers. You need to pass them out and add a personal touch, and that means everyone from your sales team to the cashier.

Initially, you may not see many certificates returned because the reality is most people will throw them away instead of passing them along. Of those who do receive one of the gift certificates from one of your current customers, a certain percentage will likely lose them.

Even so, that does not mean the strategy isn't working. Your customers are significantly more likely to refer a friend because of what you are doing and will refer more people because they are thinking about it. The key is to measure new customers and not just returned certificates.

From a practical perspective, it is important the certificate does not look like a coupon which is handed out to everyone or mailed to all homes. Gift certificates are purchased, so in people's minds they have greater value. Have enough gift certificates printed so that you can give one to nearly every customer who comes in over a month's time.

Most certificates should be handed out after the completion of a sale or payment of services so it doesn't seem like a hard sell. Or you can have the cashier be the point person for transactions not involving a salesman.

You can hire an outside company to design the certificates or do it yourself in-house. However, I think it's better to go to a local printer because normally the print quality won't be professional quality if printed in-house unless you happen to own a commercial grade printer.

Promotional Items

Just about any item can have a business name or logo printed on it: pens, hats, t-shirts, coffee mugs, balloons, key chains, flash drives, complimentary bottled water, bumper stickers, window decals, reusable bags, notepads, and even candy. While this type of marketing may be more passive, these items go a long way to keeping your business's brand top of mind within your customer base.

When using any graphics such as a photograph, an illustration, or line art, make sure you have the necessary permissions to use them if not created in-house or by a hired graphic artist.

Sponsorships

Goodwill can be a powerful, albeit indirect, marketing tool. For example, starting in 2007, Enterprise Rent-a-Car partnered with the Arbor Day Foundation and the United States Forest Service to plant one million trees every year for 50 years in America, Canada, and Europe to restore areas damaged by fires, weather, or disease, as well as to expand natural habitats for endangered species. Similarly, in the United Kingdom, supermarket giant, Sainsbury is well known for sponsoring the London 2012 Paralympics.

That kind of philanthropy can attract customers who want to reward the company.

On a local or regional scale, sponsoring a youth sports team or league, community projects, the arts or being active in the community can result in new customers as well as increased loyalty. Sponsorship is not just for the 'big guns with deep pockets'. Many small businesses sponsor local sports teams and community events and receive increased profile in their local market as a result. Also, if your business is known for sponsoring something that your potential customer feels passionate about, the customer feels more empathy towards your business, and could make a buying decision to buy from you because of the sponsorship link.

Internet Marketing

Internet marketing has evolved significantly in recent years as consumers increasingly research, shop, and purchase goods and services online. The best known tool is search engine optimization (SEO), where key words are used for recognition by search engines such as Google and Yahoo, Firefox, and many others.

Another popular strategy is article marketing, where businesses regularly publish articles relevant to their products or services on their website. The articles provide readers with informative content and provide links for search engine crawlers to categorize. The same is true of blogs, which are the digital equivalent to 'To the Editor' letters in daily newspapers.

Just as direct marketing mail remains alive and well, especially among local businesses such as grocery stores and car dealerships, email marketing is also ubiquitous. Email blasts can reach a large audience without any additional financial investment beyond an internet service and are effective at keeping a business top of mind among consumers. Companies like Fresh and Easy and World Market send out weekly emails that include coupons and news of in-store sales to prod customers to stop by.

Facebook and Twitter may have started as a way to keep tabs on friends and let them know what you're doing, but these social networks are among the most powerful online marketing tools around. While still in its relative infancy as a marketing tool, small and large businesses are embracing Business Facebook by creating company web pages for consumers to 'like' and therefore get all their updates. As more of our world moves online, marketing techniques using Facebook, Twitter, Pinterest, and Google+ will develop and proliferate. The great thing about this type of marketing is that the playing field is level. Your business can be just you, yet you have the same ability to market as the bigger players in your market via the internet.

Social media sites such as LinkedIn provide a way to target specific demographics as well as offering instant interaction with customers. LinkedIn also provides opportunities for you to demonstrate your expertise via blogs and article writing to draw in a potential customer base to you and your personal brand.

Social media is the 'new way' of marketing, and is scary and exciting all at once as it is so immediate and new. Regardless of how you feel about it as a business owner, you need to embrace it as it is the way of the future, and if you do not, you will get left behind.

I know of one hotel manager who responds to every comment left by a guest, good or bad. Letting customers know their opinion counts goes a long way toward building loyalty and repeat business.

Networking

Businesses depend on customers to survive. While advertising and marketing strategies are a tried and true strategy to attract new customers, their effectiveness is inconsistent and marketing can be expensive. Smart entrepreneurs use all the tools at their disposal, and one of the most powerful tools is you.

I personally think that networking is one of the best ways in which businesses can grow as nothing beats face to face contact. Networking enables you to make business to business connections because it gives you the chance to let people know about your business and accumulate referrals and potential affiliates. Some of the most effective places to network include Business Networking International or BNI, the internationally renowned referral organization that I am a member of, Chambers of Commerce, Rotary and Lions, community events, and even volunteering for local charity events.

Developing Referral Partners

A referral partner is someone who will refer your business to their customers when their customers have a need for your products and services. Referral partnerships are the 'gold dust' of networking in my opinion, yet probably the least understood and used by small businesses. Imagine having other businesses recommending you to their customers, and having those customers call to buy from you because of the strength of the reputation you have with your referral partner. Who would not want that type of referral partner?

I am always suggesting to my clients that they build relationships with referral partners, firstly by identifying suitable referral partner businesses, being clear about the value proposition they offer customers, and then slowly building the relationship with the referral partner, passing their business potential customers when the opportunity arises. If a strong business, professional and personal relationship develops between you and your referral partner, they will pass potential customers your way all day long, as it makes them look good and helpful — offering added value to their customers by referring them to someone they respect and trust in business. Examples of perfect referral partnerships include:

- Carpeting/flooring contractors building referral business partner relationships with property developers, realtors/ estate agents, and interior designers.
- Book keepers building referral business partner relationships with accountants who don't do book keeping.
- Human resources consultants building referral business partner relationships with employment attorneys/lawyers, accountants, and business coaches.
- Business coaches building referral business partner relationships with accountants and corporate attorneys/ lawyers.
- Massage therapists building referral business partner relationships with fitness instructors, hair salons, doctors, dentists, and complementary alternative health practitioners.
- Photographers building referral business partner relationships with events managers and function centers, hair salons, wedding dress sellers, florists, and jewelry shops.
- Builders building referral business partner relationships with realtors/ estate agents, property developers, and other business owners in the trades.

For every business in every sector, there are natural business referral partnerships.

Finding Cheerleaders
Every business has cheerleaders, people who will sing from the

rooftops about the products and services of the business. Cheerleaders are also 'gold dust' when it comes to finding new customers. For cheerleaders to continue cheerleading about your business, they need to be nurtured and updated on what is occurring in your business, so it is important to continue to effectively communicate with those people.

Affiliate Marketing

Online affiliate marketing, which is the whole premise of Google's AdWords, is another way to create customers for your business. Affiliate marketing is performance based, where businesses can monetise their website by earning commissions for promoting an advertiser.

Cold Calling

A more traditional strategy that can still be effective is cold calling, not so much to close a deal but for gathering information or trying to get an in-person appointment to better explain your product or service. Cold-calling is one of those things that people either love or hate to do — it polarises most business people. Large businesses use this tool to telephone potential customers from lists they create. Smaller businesses can use this method too.

Personally I have never minded calling people, and in my consulting business I had significant success in making contact with the person I wanted to speak to and arranging an appointment to meet with them to discuss the consulting services offered by my company. At those meetings, I would then properly present my business credentials while finding out more about the potential customer, and often that first meeting was the start of a very long business association.

So Many Options

All of the above techniques have their strengths and weaknesses, and what is the best method for one business or industry may not be right for another. The key to securing new customers is to select and perfect the marketing tool that best suits you as the business owner, your business and the industry you are a part of.

❗ There are many marketing tools to attract potential customers. All businesses should implement a series of marketing initiatives.

Marketing vs Sales

Marketing and sales are obviously interdependent in many ways. A business's success ultimately depends on convincing enough customers to buy its products or services. A business can only grow as much as its sales allow. Marketing is a tool for assuring future sales through attracting new customers and holding onto current ones. In order for consumers to spend money at your business, they need to know that it exists, what products it offers, and the value of those products. Marketing's purpose is bringing customers into your business in person, to your website online, or calling you on the telephone. In other words, marketing is the first step of the sales process, which ends with the customer buying a product or service.

Marketing encompasses a broad range of activities including researching what products or services consumers want, producing quality products, pricing, promoting, and selling the product or service to consumers.

Despite its importance, many small businesses skimp on marketing. The most common reason given is money. Owners of new or small businesses that are working on low margins and tight cash flow feel they cannot afford to devote financial resources on the luxury of marketing.

But the reality is without marketing the likelihood of a business succeeding or reaching its potential is significantly reduced. Marketing is how a company generates new customers, whether through advertising, product samples, joining networking groups or other strategies, as well as how a business keeps those customers via branding and reputation. Marketers pay special attention to customer attitudes and the trends of their product and service choices.

The best way to incorporate marketing is to integrate its costs within your overall yearly business plan. Determine if and when you'll need to spend money on things like special promotions, new product launches, or advertising. Be creative in your marketing approach and identify the best ways to attract business, be it signage, direct mail, brochures, demonstrations, or joint promotions. Once you have laid out your strategy, then your marketing investment will be part of your operating expenses. The key is to maximise your marketing dollars so you don't waste money but still get full value from your efforts.

Industrial marketing strategist Kerry O'Malley notes that effective marketing not only helps to increase sales, it also creates one of a company's most valuable assets — a recognisable brand. "An integrated marketing communications plan that gets your messaging out to the right target audience, consistently and over time, will eventually create the *top of mind* awareness for your product or service that turns a prospect into a customer. If you're keeping your company's name out there and building brand identity and recognition, you have less of an educational process to deal with every time a new person is introduced to your business."

Another benefit is that satisfied customers will send referrals as well as create perceived value. O'Malley notes, "It takes more than the experiences with your company to make a satisfied customer; it also takes a marketing strategy that positions your company in the minds of your target audience as the market leader in overall customer satisfaction."

Marketing also levels the playing field by allowing new or smaller businesses to compete against established or larger companies. Without a targeted marketing plan, it would be nearly impossible for entrepreneurs to gain a foothold in their particular industry or marketplace.

There is no shortcut to marketing; it is a long-term commitment and investment. But without it, you won't be able to create a recognizable brand, which in turn will hinder your company's ability to grow a successful business.

But it is important to make sure that everyone in your business is on board with your brand and your strategies on gaining and maintaining customers. To that end, I'd suggest using all the feedback you receive from customers — whether verbally, on social media, or via questionnaires — as a reference and a resource. It should be collected, catalogued, and then made available to every employee to establish a company culture that is based on creating the best customer experience possible.

A Final Word

It is critical to be very clear about what is expected from your employees when it comes to promoting customer experience. This may mean holding workshops, especially if trying to incorporate *hot button* strategies, so there is consistency. It's also important to explain why customer experience is so crucial to the company's success because that understanding hopefully leads to increased staff engagement with customers, which over time should lead to increased sales.

The benefits of prioritising customer experience may not immediately show up on the company's bottom line but it will pay long-term dividends. No amount of advertising can equal the power of positive word of mouth and a reputation built on top customer experience.

Research shows that businesses that make customer experience a priority enjoy significant revenue and reputation benefits. In today's extremely crowded marketplace, consistently delivering positive customer experiences is an invaluable competitive advantage.

Adèle McLay, the Agitator
Many small business owners believe that marketing is for big businesses, and that they can't afford to market their business. In fact, small business owners cannot afford NOT to market their business in the crowded market place. In my opinion, a lack of marketing leads to almost certain death of the business over time. What strategies does your business have in place to ensure a constant flow of potential customers are learning more about your business and its products and services?

 ## Strategy 11

Finding 'Lots More' Customers
Marketing is crucial to long-term business success, as all businesses need a constant flow of potential customers to present their business to.

Select the marketing options that suit you (the business owner), your staff, your business and your industry, create a structured marketing plan, and effectively implement it.

Marketing delivers results over the long-term and supports brand awareness of your business.

Failure to consistently market your business will often result in reduced business, which over time could lead to the demise of the business.

Samantha Rathling

CEO of Recruitment Magic, Business Mentor, Best-Selling Author and International Speaker

Samantha decided at a young age that she wanted to own her own business by age 30, so started her working career in marketing, moving into sales, to get the broadest experience she could ahead of achieving that goal. A chance move into the recruitment industry while living in The Netherlands and she found her passion, a career she really loved and was very good at. Upon moving to the Republic of Ireland, Samantha decided to establish her own recruitment company, so achieved her goal of being self employed two years ahead of her original schedule.

The recruitment industry is cluttered in most countries, and Ireland is no different. Sam quickly realised she needed to find a niche that was different to the +80 local competitors, and needed to network to grow her business. Walt Disney's quote, "*Observe the masses and do the opposite*" resonated with Sam, so she created a unique selling proposition and niche that was customer-centric and different from her competition, and then she learnt the art of effective networking. It worked as Sam has a thriving business, even now during the Global Financial Crisis that has decimated much of Ireland's industry.

Personal and company branding has been critical to the success of Sam's business. Reputation is everything to Sam, both face-to-face and online. She believes that one has to become the 'go-to expert in what you do' so that when a potential customer needs a particular product or service, they go to your business, because it is the first one they think of.

Sam's key learnings in business to date are: play to your strengths and '*delegate, automate or eliminate*'; get a business coach, someone who will hold you to account and offer an external perspective; and surround yourself with successful people.

Sam's key advice to budding entrepreneurs is: 1) Keep your overheads low, manage your cash flow, and if you are not good at numbers, then get good at numbers. 2) Have a clear vision for the business, and perhaps create a vision board to help you remember what you want to achieve, something you can refer to if the going gets tough. 3) Go for it! She says, "even though you are a small business, it doesn't mean that you can't win big contracts". Sam herself achieved that by leveraging her networks.

Sam has developed a second business called Elite for Business, where she will personally mentor 10 VIP clients annually to assist them to halve the hours they work in their business while doubling their profits. Sam only works 20 hours per week now as she has three young children, so she is practising what she preaches!

Adèle's Note: I have known Sam for several years, and she is hugely respected and networked around the world. She is a huge 'giver' to others, and has become known as a 'Givingpreneur'; she has written a book of the same name, which was a best-seller. Sam believes the more one gives in business and life, the more one gets in return, and I endorse that view and live that life also. Sam is an inspiration to many and will continue to build her profile and career, and will enjoy ongoing business success in light of her approach to business and life.

To connect with Samantha Rathling:
W: www.eliteforbusiness.com
    www.samrathling.com
    www.recruitmentmagic.com
Tw: @samrathling
FB: Sam Rathling
LIn: Sam Rathling
YT: Sam Rathling

Chapter 9

How McDonald's Beat The System

The first rule of any technology used in a business is that automation applied to an efficient operation will magnify the efficiency. The second is that automation applied to an inefficient operation will magnify the inefficiency. **Bill Gates**

I just love the Bill Gates' quote. It's so true. In my consulting and coaching work, time and time again I have worked with small businesses in relative chaos as they have not grasped the importance of systems and automation to make their own job easier. However, I have also worked with very small businesses where they are fully systemised and automated as 'one-man-bands', yet they look and feel bigger from a customer's point of view as they are so professional and seamless. Those systemised businesses are ready to grow their staff when the time is right, and new staff will easily slot into the systemised business.

You might be thinking, "What has a systemised and automated business got to do with *Big Profits?*" A business's operations are the heart and soul of its business because they derive value from assets and require making ongoing improvements so your company can achieve and maintain a competitive advantage. There is a fine line between creativity and chaos. In my experience, a well thought-out, structured operations strategy built on smart systems means less energy is expended putting out fires and more energy is devoted to improving the business and its value. Such efficiencies set a firm foundation for growth and increased profits.

Ensuring my clients have robust and reliable systems in place in their businesses is one of the many ways I *agitate* them to achieve more success in their business. I cannot overestimate the importance of having systems in place in businesses. In the technology driven world we live in today, automation of business systems and processes is achievable and affordable. Also, using outsourcing as a tool to enable systems to be put in place and run effectively in the business is another way in which small businesses can enhance the efficiency and perceived professionalism of their business.

Business Systems

A business system is a group of processes that collectively work to deliver the same result. A process is the step-by-step template of tasks that need to be done in a certain order, to reach a desired outcome. An operation that runs on systems is the Holy Grail of all businesses — big and small. Systemisation means taking business processes out of the owner's heads and establishing procedures that cut reliance on key people and improve automation and product quality. Businesses need to use technology to reduce or eliminate manual tasks and processes, develop step by step manuals, or create an automated system that enables others to accomplish the needed processes.

Systems provide stability. Businesses without systems tend to be more volatile, which means they carry more inherent risk. A stable business is a lower risk. Like stability, consistency is important for any business. Smart systems take average people and make them smart by delivering desired results consistently. It can also let you determine the true business value. Consistency is sustainability which leads to business profits and hopefully *Big Profits*.

Businesses with carefully implemented systems are significantly more efficient and by that I mean operations run with very little resources or attention. An example of a business with efficient systems would be In-N-Out Burger or McDonald's. These businesses are well known internationally for their efficiency in making burgers to a system for their customers.

Another aspect of systemising is standardisation, where every customer, vendor, and supplier gets the same quality of experience every time. Any business that becomes franchised has strong systems that can be easily and efficiently replicated because the end game is to have systems run the business and people run the systems.

The point is that if your business depends on a couple of key people who have everything inside their head, and one drops dead and the other gets a cold, your business will shut down and you can forget about getting any kind of a premium for your business if it has to be sold. That's a case of you not owning the business; the business owns you.

When someone says their business is having growing pains, what they really mean is, "We've done everything out of our head and when we were small it was easy. But as we got bigger and had to hire new people, that information did not get relayed well, and so we started dropping the ball."

Take a business that provides a service like website design. At first he takes care of his customers just fine even though there are no systems in place because it's easy for the owner to remember the customers and it's easy to follow up with everybody. But then he starts getting more and more referrals and he can't remember everything anymore so things start to fall through the cracks, and over time the chances are high that the business will fail. But by systemising his business, the website designer creates a process that describes how to handle the different elements of his business. And now he can hand jobs off to a new employee who can manage that work by following the system.

Think of it as creating a recipe. When you are baking a cake, you follow a process or system. Generally the sugar and butter are beaten thoroughly together first, then the eggs are added and beaten in. The dry ingredients are added and are 'folded' in; being folded in is an important part of the system, because, depending on the cake you are making, if you beat the dry ingredients in, you will end up with a flat, airless cake. You see, even cake baking follows a system.

In restaurants, they'll often take a photograph of what the plate presentation is supposed to look like so as the chef prepares the food they know that's what they'll be measured against.

Author Joerg Sieber notes: "If you ever run into a business owner who is not stressed out about the operations of his or her company, chances are he or she has the necessary structures and processes in place that help the business run without chaos and frantic emergencies. A structured and systemised business offers many advantages to a business owner and the entire team in the company."

Those benefits include:

- Structure.
- Stability.
- Control.
- Reduced stress.
- Efficiency.
- Effectiveness.
- Motivation.

The rest of this chapter offers some practical and essential tools that will help establish business processes in all parts of a business. These suggestions are designed to make operations a well-oiled machine with minimal problems and provide a proven system to identify and fix any problems that do arise.

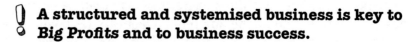 **A structured and systemised business is key to Big Profits and to business success.**

Sales Processes

It's important to establish a sales process designed to identify leads and then turn them into customers. Rather than have each sales person develop their own processes which they alone follow, it is much more effective to develop a clearly defined system for everyone to follow. The first step is to target areas to find leads. For example, if you own a roofing business, networking with local commercial and residential builders would make sense, as they could be your *referral partners* as we discussed in Chapter 8. You could also go to DIY expos, set up a booth and speak to homeowners looking to replace or repair their roofs.

If you are a veterinarian opening a new practice, you might want to network at a local dog show or even volunteer at an animal shelter in exchange for them handing out flyers or brochures about your practice.

Whatever your business, you need to identify the businesses and individuals that are most likely to generate strong leads and prospective customers. As previously noted, in some cases, you might generate leads networking at functions, or you might do it via social networks, or the old-fashioned way through advertising and making telephone calls.

Once you have the leads you can set your process in motion. One strategy is to start by building a database to keep track of each lead; who you contacted, when you contacted them, the products or services you provide that the potential customer can use, and when you need to follow-up — it's important to be persistent without being pushy because just staying in contact eventually builds relationships that can turn into business.

Research shows that very often it takes seven contact points with a lead before a sale is made, yet many businesses give up on that potential customer after about two or three contacts with them, thinking they aren't interested. In fact, it might be that they are just not interested right now, but may need your products and services later. So, if you don't have a system to connect with those potential customers over and over again, then you are likely to discard them and lose them.

Whatever the specifics of the system you develop, it should complement your particular product or service, and be written down so everyone involved will be on the same page. Your lead tracking system can be as simple as a basic Excel file, or a sophisticated customer management system. This tool is so important for businesses and has a multitude of uses, tracking potential customers as well as showing which marketing strategy generated which lead. Tracking that information is important too as over time it will provide patterns of success in lead and conversion generation for your business, so that your business can focus its marketing and networking systems on those areas that generate most success.

 All businesses need a lead generation strategy.

Marketing Plans

Any marketing plan should outline a business's strategies on how to generate new leads and customers such as through advertising, product samples, or social media campaigns. Author Joerg Sieber stresses, "No marketing plan without specific action items will help you get to your goals. In other words, simply listing the marketing strategies you want to implement is not enough. In addition to listing the strategies, develop a clear action plan on how to implement each strategy, and then list each action item in a marketing calendar so you can systematically implement each strategy and track."

Marketing is for all businesses.

Business Plans

The United States Small Business Administration says a business plan is important because it "precisely defines your business, identifies your goals, and serves as your firm's resumé. It helps you allocate resources properly, handle unforeseen complications, and make the right decisions. Because it provides specific and organised information about your company and how you will repay borrowed money, a good business plan is a crucial part of any loan package. Additionally, it can tell your sales personnel, suppliers, and others about your operations and goals."

In others words, a business plan is vital to establishing and maintaining robust operations. It tells you who you are, where you are going, and how you plan to get there. The specific content of a business plan varies depending on the business, although there are some standard elements.

Why are business plans important in making *BIG Profits*? If you have not written down what you want to achieve in business along with how you are going to achieve it, then you will not achieve it. It is as simple as that.

 A planned and systematic approach to business leads to BIG Profits.

Operations Manuals

For many small businesses, the only operations manual they have is tucked inside the brain of the entrepreneur founder of the company. When there is only an employee or two, it's easy enough for the owner to explain how he wants things to run. But as the business grows there needs to be a written document that details all the specific information needed to run the company. In addition to being an effective way of communicating policy and procedures to employees so they can get maximum results in their positions, it's also practical if you ever need to hire a temporary employee to fill in for a vacationing employee or one that's left the business without warning.

The operations manual, according to business coach Joerg Sieber, "is a crucial and ever-changing document that enables the owner of a company to grow the business to the point where he or she is no longer required to be available for questions 24/7. An Operations Manual is needed if you ever want to duplicate your company."

The contents of the operations manual will be company specific but in general should include:

- Company history.
- Vision and organisation structure.
- Job descriptions.
- How-to instructions.
- Products & services.
- Policies.
- Action plans.

You can organise the manual into two sections: information that all employees need to know, and information that is position-specific, meaning you should create a manual for every job position in your business. To start, you need to identify every position, their assigned duties or tasks, any standards they need to comply to, and what resources or materials they need to do their job.

The Wall Street Journal Complete Small Business Guidebook notes: "Every operations manual is different, so there's no exact formula to follow. You'll want to create one that essentially maps out exactly how things get done in your specific business. For instance, how do you like customers to be greeted when they come in the door; or what day of the month do you order supplies from a vendor? Where do you keep the extra set of keys to the storage room? The operations manual, essentially, is a tool kit for replicating your knowledge of your business and what you do on any given day."

The Wall Street Journal also suggests, "As your business grows, you may wish to have separate manuals for different departments or divisions. You might also develop a basic version for entry-level employees and a more detailed version (with sensitive information on finances, for example) for senior managers."

Another important area is IT and technology. Remember to include all the business's devices, computers, and software employed to run the business. Include passwords and contact information for website servers needed to update online content and renew domain names.

It's easy to put off writing an operations manual when you are spending your day actually doing the work but it is a piece of operational insurance you can't afford not to do. As Janine Popick, CEO and founder of Vertical Response says bluntly, "Start making it a policy now to get your people to start documenting what they do and how they do it so you're not in trouble if they're not around."

It's also important to keep the operations handbook current. Businesses evolve so the business's manuals should be reviewed every six months to ensure they are up to date. One efficient way to do this is to let each manager review the manual so they can make any needed updates and additions.

Some owners find it difficult to relinquish all the knowledge of running a business. But the ultimate goal should be having a business that can run without you having to be there every second to make sure its operations are running effectively. And if you ever want to sell your business, having a detailed operations manual will be integral to a smooth transition of ownership.

Inspired by Michael Gerber's book, The *E-Myth*, when establishing my New Zealand based consulting business, I created processes and systems for everything we did in the business. Once the manuals were established the operations and support staff regularly updated them; they became known as the '*McLay Way*' manuals and were central to the business being able to grow systematically over time. The manuals also formed part of the induction process for all new employees. We were very clear within the business that we wanted all our clients to enjoy a seamless and systematic experience, so they knew what to expect. The consultants could then stamp their own personalities onto the '*McLay Way*' system as they developed the relationships with our customers.

 Operations processes and supporting manuals are critical to all businesses.

Financial Systems

As much as it distresses me to say this as a Chartered Accountant, in my experience, the importance a small business places on financial systems often depends on the level of confidence and experience the business owner has 'with the numbers'. In many small businesses, finances are not actively controlled and managed, often causing the business to lurch from one financial crisis to the next.

At the very least, all businesses should have a budgeted cash flow, and that should be monitored as a priority as we learnt in Chapter Two. The harsh reality is, without positive cash flow, combined with profitability, a business will not survive for long. So a fundamental aspect of financial control is managing those two integral parts of the business's operations. To do this effectively requires a system that keeps track of your business's objectives along with measurements of specific procedures such as what controls will be over expenses. Even the smallest change in either costs or sales will have a significant impact on profits, which are defined as the difference between sales and costs.

The first step to devise a system is to develop a financial plan along with a process for monitoring your business's performance against the plan's objectives. It is vital to keep accurate records for several reasons, the most obvious being for tax and legal purposes. The records should be detailed enough that you can tell how much cash the business is bringing in, how much you owe your creditors, how much is owed to you, and your current profit margins. Other aspects of your control method can include:

- A computerised book keeping system.
- Regularly reviewed budgets.
- Regular financial reports which include comparisons to budget.
- Monthly reconciling of bank accounts.
- Inventory reviews and work-in-progress.
- Documented operational policies.
- Fraud protections.

Maintaining a strong financial control system keeps a business on track with its objectives, establishes a warning system if expenses creep too high, and provides information on whether to expand or downsize a business.

Ideally all small businesses should have a book keeper, either contracted or on the staff, who inputs all business transactions into a computerised system for review within the month or at month-end. If a business owner is not comfortable with the financial management of their business, then to ensure the owner has full control of the business, rather than it controlling them, the services of a good accountant — preferably one who does management accounting — should be employed. A good accountant or business adviser is worth their weight in gold to a small business owner, as they can produce and interpret the monthly financial accounts, so they can be reviewed with the business owner and the business tweaked to improve its performance. It is too late reviewing the annual accounts that are prepared for tax purposes after the end of the financial year, as they are historic at that point.

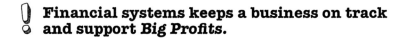 **Financial systems keeps a business on track and support *Big Profits*.**

Job Descriptions

A job description explains the reason for and function of the position, plus various aspects of what will be expected of the applicant. It should list responsibilities, skill sets and professional qualifications needed, and intangible attributes required to flourish.

Ideally, a job description should read like a table of contents and include:

- Title.
- Department.

- Immediate superior.
- Key areas of responsibility.
- Qualifications and experience required.
- Educational requirements, if any; in most cases, real world job experience is considered comparable to an academic certification or degree.
- Special skills, anything from knowing a foreign language or having specific technological know-how.
- Physical requirements, should the job entail heavy lifting, long periods standing or driving.

The advantage of a well-written job description is you get more appropriate applicants and better prepared new employees who can start contributing immediately.

> **When employing staff, all businesses should have job descriptions to aid the employee.**

Performance Management Systems

Small businesses don't always think they need performance management, especially if they only have a few employees. But it is preferable to establish a performance management system from the start so it is already in place as your business grows and/or diversifies. Performance management is used to evaluate an employee and helps determine the merit of remuneration raises and promotions; it raises red flags if a team member's productivity starts falling; and informs employees of what is expected from them.

> **Performance management systems are easily implemented in all businesses — big and small.**

Employee Handbooks

There was a time when it was standard operating procedure for new employees to undergo a formal orientation that inundated them with materials such as a tour of the office; introductions to the people in their new department or on their assigned team; a call directory; an organisation chart; a one-on-one lunch with the manager; and a meeting with Human Resources (if the company was big enough) to discuss the specifics of the employee manual. This process typically lasted up to a week in larger businesses.

However, smaller businesses are often more casual in their orientation system, with some opting for a sink-or-swim approach. But while some managers may see this as a test of the new employee's initiative, in reality it's counterproductive and likely to leave the new employee overwhelmed.

Those small businesses that do have an orientation often cover everything in a matter of hours. After the initial orientation, it is up to the employee to figure things out. But it takes even the best of workers time to adjust and get the 'lay of the land'. As a result, employee manuals are taking on an increasingly important role in many businesses, says career coach Lynn Desert.

"These documents lay down the basic rules for all employees. Most employee manuals are standardised and only require a little bit of customisation by each company. They include topics such as work hours, sick and vacation time, standards of behavior, reprimand and reward systems. Employees have to sign a copy of this manual and thus communicate that they are aware of company policies and procedures. Employee manuals can be lifesavers if issues arise between employees and companies."

Because they are so specific, one size definitely does not fit all when it comes to employee handbooks. Each one needs to be unique for each specific business. When done correctly, handbooks can be used as a primer that sets the business tone because all the workers are literally on the same page. It removes ambiguity regarding policy and rules over a wide variety of issues, including personal cell phone or computer usage at work, attendance, overtime, tardiness, social media restrictions, and any areas of confidentiality.

Handbooks can also cover dress codes; fraternisation policies, if any; complaint procedures; vacation time; and any incentive initiatives. In short, consider them the company's commandments; a resource employees can refer back to time and again.

They also offer consistency — few things set the stage for internal strife more than employees being given differing rules or boundaries by different managers. The best employee handbooks will be informative, unambiguous, and to the point. Keep the content concise, on-point, and written in a user-friendly style. This isn't a court brief. Use language everyone can understand.

By having rules and policies written out, it lets your employees know exactly what is expected from them and what they can expect in the workplace. Employee handbooks can also offer a layer of legal protection should a disgruntled employee ever file a claim against you, especially if you require employees signing that they have read the handbook, understand its contents, and agree to abide by the rules and policies therein.

 Employee handbooks are critical for business success.

Job Onboarding

Onboarding, also known as organisational socialisation, is the process by which new employees learn the training, skills, and behaviours to successfully integrate into a new job, thereby becoming a productive and valuable company asset.

A leadership white paper entitled *Hiring For Attitude: Research & Tools to Sky Rocket Your Success Rate* by Mike Murphy asserts that 46 percent of new employees fail within the first 18 months and only 19 percent of them achieve success in their new roles. It was not their skill set that most often failed; it was attitude.

Career Coach Lynn Desert explains, "Successful onboarding socialises new employees and prevents attitudinal or interpersonal behavior problems that can lead to early dismissal or departure. During the process new employees are introduced to success factors required to become functioning and productive employees including knowledge, skills, behaviors, and attitudes."

Businesses that work with and support new employees will reap the benefits of smoother operations and a more efficient workplace. Here are some ways to help new employees acclimatise:

- Encourage early communication with new employees; have managers and human resources contact them by telephone to welcome them aboard.
- Establish internal social media sites so new employees can introduce themselves to their co-workers.
- Create a 30/60/90-day plan that outlines initial goals and measurable benchmarks for the first three months on the job.
- Make sure the employee has all the resources they need to do their job including technology hardware and software.
- Offer a mentoring program with key people within the organisation.
- Have an open door policy for ideas and suggestions.
- Be realistic; give the employee time to reach their stride.

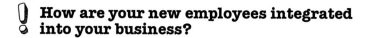 **How are your new employees integrated into your business?**

Automation

Automating your business as much as possible is critical to gain and maintain a competitive advantage, which increases value for both your customer and your business. It also means the business owner can spend more time working on their business rather than fighting fires within it.

By developing systems, operational problems can be recognised, identified, and addressed as soon as they happen. Often operational issues can be resolved by automating parts of the process to make it more streamlined for staff and customers alike.

Let me give you an example of a perfectly systemised small business. Geoff is an electrician who grasps how, by automating his business, his downtime doing paperwork is minimised. When a customer calls to arrange a visit, the appointment is booked into a cloud based appointment system. An appointment confirmation is automatically sent by email or text, and a reminder of the appointment is made a day before, and then two hours before, and is automated. When Geoff attends the customer's site, if a quote is required, he does it there and then via his tablet computer using a job costing system that is appropriate to his industry. He carries a portable printer in his motor vehicle so the quote is given immediately. If accepted, he does the job on the nominated day as scheduled by the cloud appointment system; any further appointments are handled in the same way. When the job is complete the invoice is prepared on the spot via the tablet computer, printed and given to the customer, who knows in advance that payment is required on the day. Geoff has a portable debit/credit card processing machine, so processes the payment, and gives the customer a receipt. The online invoice details are automatically captured by Geoff's accounting system which can produce daily, weekly, monthly financial information on the productivity and profitability of Geoff's business along with tax return information. Geoff has a financial adviser who receives the same information, and together they review the performance of his business, making changes to the business model as necessary to improve financial performance. Geoff has a fully automated business.

That type of automation model can be applied to many other small businesses if the business owner gets the right support and guidance.

 Systems and automation: a business cannot survive without them.

Adèle McLay, the Agitator

My friend and interviewee in this book, Samantha Rathling, says that a business owner has to play to their strengths by "*delegating, automating or eliminating*". I totally agree with this sentiment. How is your business operating — semi or fully automated or manually operated, requiring you to spend a lot of administration time in the business?

Administration time is down time, and a waste of time, when you could be using that time to find and service new and existing customers.

How about talking to suitable advisers about how to create business systems in your business and automate as many of the systems as possible, so when you are ready to leap to the next phase in your business's growth, your business is also ready?

Strategy 12

Business Systems and Automation are the Key to Big Profits

Manual processes and a system-less business are a waste of a business owner's precious time and leads to an ad hoc approach to business, rather than a consistently applied approach.

All elements of business can be systemised: sales and marketing processes; operations processes; planning processes; financial processes; and employment and performance management processes.

Even a business that employs the owner only should be systemised as if it were the prototype for a franchised business. In doing so, the business operates efficiently and consistently for the benefit of all customers, staff and the business owner.

Rick Tobin

Owner/Broker, Premier Hotel Realty in Florida

Prior to establishing his own business, Premier Hotel Realty, Rick worked in a number of other industries and jobs which supported him to become 'well rounded, persistent and flexible'. Rick commented that with each market change he has lived and worked through, there has always been an opportunity for him, because he looked for it and was flexible in his approach. Three years ago Rick established his own business as a hotel sales broker, working with investors and sellers of hotels across the world. Regardless of the global financial crisis in full swing at the time, Rick decided to 'do it anyway'; he wanted to follow his dream and make it work.

Rick's biggest fear when starting out was whether there would be enough business in his niche market to survive. Again, he had to be flexible in his approach to the new business, so rather than relying on banks to fund the deals for investors, he focused on seeking out investors who did not need to borrow to invest.

Marketing properties for sale is second nature to Rick, but what he needed, was access to investors, so he focused his marketing efforts on networking — in person and online. He is a heavy user of LinkedIn and business Facebook to build his business's international profile in the online business community. He also joined his local BNI group and uses their online membership tools to connect with members across the world. As he sources investors from across the world, Rick is a considerable user of other technology, including Skype, Dropbox, SkyDrive, Google Docs and more to work with his clients – both investors and sellers.

Rick has worked hard to differentiate his business from others in his niche. Techniques include: global marketing; collaboration with other brokers to ensure the right investor is found for a property; and guaranteeing customer satisfaction, something that can be a real challenge to achieve in any industry.

The key lessons Rick has learnt in his career to date include: the importance of setting clear and specific goals and plans to achieve those goals; concentrating on getting the job done — clients want results, they are not looking for friends; to listen and listen again to his clients to ensure he fully understands their goals so he can help his clients achieve them. Finally, Rick believes that is it important to be positive and to 'look for the good in every situation because it is always there'.

Rick has personal coaches and mentors who support him, and he listens to and learns from well known professional gurus like Anthony Robbins, Dale Carnegie, Zig Ziglar, Michael Gerber, Mike Ferry and Dr Ivan Misner.

Rick offers budding entrepreneurs the following thoughts: 1) Listen to what your clients want; understand what their real objectives are in working with you. 2) Work with and for people you like and concentrate on your 'A' clients, not your 'B' and 'C' clients. 3) Think big! Go for it in your business!

Rick's goal over the next three to five years is to continue helping more people to live their dreams by getting them into or out of the right or wrong real estate investments. He also wants to grow his own sales team to help them achieve massive success in their own careers. Rick believes he is living his dream at present and it is getting better and better, both professionally and personally.

Adèle's Notes: I have not met Rick. He was recommended to me as a highly successful entrepreneur who is passionate about how he supports and serves his clients. In interviewing him, I could feel his passion for what he does and the difference he has made in the lives of this clients. Rick's joy and enthusiasm are infectious, and I have no doubt that his attitude to life and business has substantially contributed to his success. Rick was a delight and inspiration to interview, and I can't wait to meet him one day.

To connect with Rick:
W: www.PremierHotelRealty.com
FB: Premier Hotel Realty
LIn: www.linkedin.com/company/Premier-Hotel-Realty

Chapter 10

Mind, Business Drivers And Soul

> Success is a journey not a destination – half the
> fun is getting there.   **Gita Bellin**

Wow, you've made it. You have got to the end of ***Small Business Huge Success*™ — *Big Profits.*** How do you feel? Exhausted? Exhilarated? Motivated? Agitated? Inspirated™? Yes, 'Inspirated™'. It is not a real word, it is my made up word which is part of my personal brand. It is part of who I am in business for my clients, *'Inspirator, Agitator, Motivator'*™.

I hope you are feeling all of those emotions in relation to your small business. Why?

I want you to feel *exhausted,* as for many readers the concepts in this book are new, and sometimes it is exhausting, reading and taking in new ideas.

I want you to feel *exhilarated,* as now you have new knowledge and strategies at your disposal, which if implemented will help you achieve *Big Profits* in your business.

I want you to feel *motivated* to continue learning and challenging yourself in relation to how you are managing your business, making changes to it by implementing some or all of the 12 strategies in this book.

I want you to feel *agitated* because while it is more work for you and your business adviser, it is worth it if it helps you to make more money in your business.

I want you to feel *inspirated*™ to continue on the path towards achieving the dream you have for your business and the lifestyle you are looking forward to as a result of your business success. Isn't the work required in your business worth it for your own success and for the life you want with your family and friends? I think it is.

I love the quote: **"Yesterday is history, tomorrow is a mystery, but today is a gift. That is why they call it the present."** — Kung Fu Panda.

Today is a gift for you; today represents the opportunity to make changes to create a more financially successful business, so that you and your family can enjoy the mysteries of tomorrow. There is no going back into history. Focus on the present and what it offers your future.

Business Drivers

In any business, there are key business drivers that support its success. Some business drivers are universal and others are company or industry specific. I am interested in those that are universal and must be monitored in all businesses to achieve the financial success desired. To achieve all that you are seeking in your small business, as the business owner somehow you must make time to work on your business, stepping back from the day to day activities of doing the work, taking time to plan and review the direction you want your business to head in, and regularly monitoring how successful you are in achieving that objective.

In summary, let's look at the key business drivers that I think are universal to all businesses and that must be actively monitored at all times.

1. Cash Flow Management — Daily, Weekly, Monthly

As we have seen in this book, in order to make *Big Profits*, cash flow management is critically important in all businesses — big and small. Positive cash flow is where there is more cash coming into the business than is being paid out, and negative cash flow is when there is more cash being paid out than is being received. Positive cash flow is the life blood of all businesses. There are many strategies available to businesses to enhance cash flow as discussed in Chapter Two. Whichever you implement in your business, ensure you keep tight control of cash flow on a daily, weekly and monthly basis according to the nature of your business. Simple spreadsheets that keep a running total of expected cash in and out of the business is more than satisfactory in a small business to keep tabs on cash flow.

2. Monthly Financial Management

A good financial adviser or accountant is worth their weight in gold to a business owner as often financial management is a weakness for a busy entrepreneur. Just be sure you employ the services of an accountant or adviser who understands management accounting. Receiving annual accounts for tax purposes is not enough for the effective management of a business. Monthly management accounts must be prepared so that the business owner can review, monitor and adjust the business as necessary during the year. At year-end, it is too late. An annual budget should be prepared before the start of a new year, along with some intra year forecasting of how the business is tracking towards achieving the budget. Key financial performance indicators that should be tracked and monitored are:

- Budgeted vs actual sales.
- Budgeted vs actual gross profit.
- Budgeted vs actual expenses (line by line).
- Budgeted vs actual net profit before tax.
- Budgeted vs actual cash flow.

In my experience, many small businesses do not have a clear understanding of the financials in relation to their business, nor do they seek advice. That can lead to their business downfall. As a business owner, make a point of understanding the basics of financial management and seek the services of a highly skilled professional who will actively support your business success.

3. Brand Management

As we learnt in Chapter Seven, brand management and perception is critically important when seeking out new customers and pricing your products and services for your customers. How is your business's brand perceived in the market? Do you know? The chances are that you do not. Perhaps it is time to think about this and clearly understand where you want to position it. Once done, you need to actively manage your brand positioning in the market. If done effectively your business will attract more of the right types of customers in your '*Lots More*' Quadrant, and you will gain clarity over how to price your products and services in support of your brand. Therefore, another key business driver is brand management and protection.

4. Marketing Management

How many potential customers do you have in your customer funnel? Your customer funnel is the pool of potential customers that you are building a relationship with, who over time might buy from your business. It can take seven or more interactions with a potential customer before they consider buying from a business. If you are not continuing to build your customer funnel with more and more business leads and referrals, your sales will dry up, and that will cause financial difficulty in your business.

Chapter Eight offers many strategies for growing your customer funnel through marketing. Whichever you select as appropriate for your business, it is important to create a marketing plan with key goals and actions to achieve those goals, put the plan into place, monitor it each week and month, and review the success of the marketing plan from a return on investment point of view to ensure whatever budget you have spent on marketing gives you an effective financial return by way of new customers.

5. Sales Management

Sales management in any business is a critical business driver. Without profitable sales, a business will not survive. Chapters

Four, Five and Seven focused on product and service profitability, customer profitability and effective pricing. A successful business — big or small — needs to know the gross margin for all its products and services in order to focus on selling more of the most profitable of those. Similarly with customers, all businesses need to have a clear understanding of customer profitability, focusing on those that are most profitable, and in my opinion, most enjoyable to work with and service.

By implementing my *L⁴ Customer Profitability Quadrant*, a small business will clearly understand the profile of its customers, and from that can create a plan to address the customers in their *'Lose Them'*, *'Look Out'*, and *'Lift Them'* quadrants, while marketing for more customers in the *'Lots More'* quadrant.

6. Customer Services Management

Customer services management is an area that very few small businesses focus on, in my opinion. Do you know how your customers perceive your business? Do they feel important to you and your business? What else might they need and want from your business?

Actually talking to customers is an underused tool — by big and small businesses. Communicating with customers and finding out their opinions can be done face to face, depending on your business, or by focus group or survey. However you do it, ongoing improvement in customer service should be an important business driver in any business. Information is power. Armed with information, what could your business do to continually improve the customer experience of your business?

Remember it is better to improve many things by 10 percent, than to focus on improving one thing by 100 percent. It is the small, often iterative enhancements to customer service and the customer experience that get noticed most and are most appreciated. Make customer service improvement a key business driver in your business.

7. Operations Management

I cannot stress enough the importance for all businesses — big and small — to have effective systems and processes in place. While the establishment of systems may take time to streamline and implement, initially taking the business owner away from the 'coal face' of the business, in the long run the benefits of a systemised business are rewarding. When the business gets to the point where it is able to recruit staff, they will be able to 'work the system', a bit like at McDonald's and other franchise businesses. A system means the business operates more efficiently and effectively for all — customers, staff, employees, suppliers and other stakeholders.

Similarly, automating manual and time consuming processes is important in achieving a nimble and responsive business.

Personally, I think that ongoing operations management improvement must be an important business driver for all businesses.

8. People Management

When a business gets to the stage that it employs staff, it is important the staff have a clear understanding of the vision for the business and their role in achieving it. If that is clearly understood, then employees will hopefully 'live and breathe it' for the owner and be an effective cheerleader for the company.

However, staff must be properly trained, managed and supported to be effective. They need a position description describing what is expected of them; they need to know how they are performing through positive and constructive feedback; and they need to be appropriately rewarded and acknowledged.

People are the most important asset a business has, so their well being and performance must be considered as a key business driver in a successful business. Systems must be put in place to support and manage staff to enable them to perform highly in their role for the greater success of the business.

Mind and Soul

I really enjoy motivational quotes, and there are many that inspire me towards all that I want to achieve in my business and personal life. One that I fundamentally agree with is: **"If you can dream it, you can do it."** — Walt Disney. That is true for anyone. The only difference between two people with a similar dream where one achieves it and the other doesn't, is mindset.

How is your mindset in relation to your business success? Do you believe you can achieve the dream you have for your business? If so, that is fantastic; you now have some new strategies to help propel you towards the business success you are seeking.

If not, why not? What is holding you back? Lack of confidence? Not enough experience? No money? Fear of failure? Family and friends not being totally supportive? Maybe it is some or all of those factors.

I want to let you into a little secret. Everyone feels fear and a lack of confidence at times. Many people and businesses struggle with a lack of money. And many people are surrounded by 'nay sayers' who are unsupportive. You are not alone. It is those who push through those boundaries, perceived limitations and setbacks towards the achievement of their dream who very often achieve it — and a lot more.

As Andy Harrington, entrepreneur and professional speaker says: **"Make your goals so big and inspiring that they make your problems seem insignificant by comparison."** There are many people in world history who had humble beginnings and who achieved their dreams in life and in business. You can be another.

Get out of your current environment and make new business contacts; surround yourself with positive people who are striving to achieve their business dream. Get networking in business groups in your local community. By surrounding yourself with positive people who have a common goal — to be successful in business — their confidence and drive will rub off on you, and will help you to achieve all that you dream of.

Keep learning. Life is about learning, and you can never learn enough in this fast changing world in which we live. If you keep learning, it opens your eyes to new ways of doing things; introduces you to people who are doing those things already and who will support you; and it will excite you as you achieve more.

There are many opportunities to learn from others who have achieved in business and life, and who share their stories and strategies towards success, along with their inspirational and motivational messages. You can access the wisdom of motivational speakers by reading their books; listening to audio recordings; watching them speak and inspire via YouTube and public appearances; by following their professional pages on Facebook; by following them on Twitter... and so it goes on. We live in the knowledge age, so I strongly encourage you to make it your life's mission to keep learning to support you to achieve your business and life dreams.

Another way to receive knowledge and support is to find a suitable business coach and/or mentor; someone who has a lot of experience in business, and who wants to positively share the benefit of that knowledge and experience with you. High quality business coaches can be expensive, but remember, very often you get what you pay for. The return of your financial investment in having a business coach can be repaid in months if not weeks if you have the right person working with you.

I hope you do more than just read this book. I hope that you will commit yourself to using the strategies to implement positive change in your business, so that you are more likely to achieve the dream you have for your business and life.

I try to live by the themes of **Dream It; Believe It; Achieve It**. This resonates with me in all that I want to achieve, personally and professionally, even when the going gets a little tough. Perhaps it does with you too. Have a big dream for your business and life; believe that it is possible; and get on with achieving it, pushing through the setbacks. Then enjoy your Small Business Huge Success.

Finally, as I have said, I love motivational quotes, so let me end this book with three further quotes that inspire me. I hope you find them inspiring and motivational too.

"You create your own universe as you go along." — Winston Churchill

"See yourself living in abundance and you will attract it." — Bob Proctor

"Life is a daring adventure or nothing." — Helen Keller

Rachelle Harte

Managing Director, Lollipop Events

Rachelle unexpectedly found herself leaving a corporate job she loved, having been with the same company for 18 years. This change in circumstance due to the need to support a family member with severe ill health meant Rachelle needed to consider her part-time employment options. After researching the market, she decided to establish an events business that focused on planning and project managing children's parties, building up a reputation in that niche before moving into other event management areas. That strategy worked, as Rachelle has been an entrepreneur for over 11 years and owns a highly successful events management business, Lollipop Events.

When establishing her business, Rachelle's initial concerns were how she differentiated herself from the local competition, and her ability to manage her business while only being able to work part-time. As a highly focused service oriented person, she wanted her business to quickly stand out in the market by growing its reputation in its niche so she could then move into a broader range of events management, so balancing her personal and work commitments was a challenge.

In the past Rachelle relied on advertising for growing her business, but in the end found advertising was not offering an effective return on investment. In recent years Rachelle has enjoyed business growth through referral marketing and collaboration. She joined a local business networking group, BNI, and that involvement has enabled her to widen her network base, support other businesses to be successful, and substantially grow her own business.

Strongly branding her business has also been a key decision for Rachelle, so that Lollipop Events is now recognised as a major events management business in South East London and beyond.

A key lesson Rachelle has learnt along her entrepreneurial pathway is that she cannot do everything herself (as much as she wants to). As an young entrepreneur, she found she was good at most things, but she continues to force herself to enlist the help and support of other professionals who complement her business, often in a mentoring way, and as a result they have helped her to grow and sustain her business for the future.

Rachelle's advice to budding entrepreneurs is: 1) Make sure everyone knows about your new venture and plans and ask them to spread the word. 2) Have a plan for what you want to achieve and keep focused on the plan. What are you here for? Where are you going? How are you going to get there? 3) Get up a little earlier each day. Even 15 minutes can make a real difference to how much you can get done when the phone is not ringing. 4) Ask for help! You will be surprised how much others want to support your success.

Rachelle's business plan includes substantially growing her corporate customer base over the next three to five years. A key area of business growth for Lollipop Events will continue to be working with local government on the regeneration of town centres in the United Kingdom, something Rachelle and her team are passionate about supporting.

Rachelle truly believes she is living her dream as an entrepreneur. She is working in an industry she loves, supporting customers to achieve their business and personal goals when hosting their event; and her company continues to substantially grow and is highly profitable.

Adèle's Notes: Rachelle is a focused, determined and very successful business woman who goes out of her way to support other businesses to achieve the success they are seeking, and in return she has built a substantial events management business herself. I have known Rachelle for several years, and have thoroughly enjoyed hearing of her ongoing business successes, and how she supports others towards their own success. Having had the privilege of using the services of Lollipop Events to manage an event of my own, I know firsthand how committed Rachelle and her team are to ensuring their clients achieve the outcomes they are seeking for their events; they definitely go beyond the call of duty in their work, and I am sure this attention to service delivery has played a major role in the success of Rachelle's business.

To connect with Rachelle:
W: www.lollipopevents.co.uk
FB: Lollipop Events

Bonuses

Thank you for reading **Small Business Huge Success**™ — **BIG Profits**. I hope you implement some or all of the 12 strategies that will support your business to make *BIG Profits*.

By visiting and registering at: www.smallbusinesshugesuccess.com/bigprofits you can gain access to free bonuses, which I hope will support you to achieve greater success in your small business.

Bonus One: Common Sizing Your Financials

Chapter Three helped you understand the importance of actively managing the expenses in your small business. In Bonus One I give you a template to download to enable you to common size your own expenses over three years. By doing that, you will easily see if you need to actively manage parts of your business.

Bonus Two: Who Are Your Most Profitable Customers?

Chapter Five asks you to rank your customers according to their profitability to your business and enjoyment. Once you have done that, you will have customers in four quadrants. Some of those customers will warrant more attention. Bonus Two is my business development template. It will help you to become very clear about the value proposition your business offers its customers and the type of customers you are seeking in the *'Lots More'* quadrant.

Bonus Three: Customer Service: How Does Your Business Rate?

Chapter Six discusses *Customer Experience Management* as defined by Bernd Schmitt. How well does your business do in providing your customers with an excellent experience so that you stand head and shoulders above your competition? Bonus Three is my special report on the key elements of customer experience management that I think all businesses should be considering in order to stand apart and to enjoy ongoing repeat business with their customers.

Bonus Four: Personal Branding

Chapter Seven looks at the importance of branding in relation to pricing. What about personal branding? What role does that play in your business? Do you know what personal branding is? Bonus Four is my special report on the importance of personal branding in business, and provides you with an introduction to the subject and the book, ***Small Business Huge Success*™ — *Personal Brand YOU!***

About Adèle McLay

Wife, Mother, Friend and Family Member; Entrepreneur; Business Adviser/ Coach; Motivational Speaker; Author; Property Investor; Ballroom/Latin Dancer; Arts Lover; Foodie/Baker; Traveller; Exercise Lover; Bridge Player; Giver... 'Inspirator, Agitator, Motivator'™ and more...

Adèle established the brand and business **Small Business Huge Success**™ due to her love of small business, and the desire to support small businesses around the world to achieve greater financial success, so business owners can live the life they dreamt about when they created the vision for their business.

Adèle passionately believes that entrepreneurs should not be a slave to their businesses, rather they need to control them, enabling the entrepreneur to enjoy a full personal and family life. Adèle leads by example, enjoying an entrepreneurial career while also enjoying her life's passions and personal interests, of which she has many.

Adèle is an experienced business adviser/coach and mentor, having advised, consulted to and coached small and large businesses and charities in New Zealand and the United Kingdom for some 20 years. She is also an experienced and inspiring public speaker and is regularly asked to speak to business groups on a range of topics related to business performance and success.

Born in New Zealand, Adèle graduated with an accounting/ finance qualification and is a Fellow Chartered Accountant of the New Zealand Institute of Chartered Accountants. Her first roles were in banking as an accountant, and later in investment banking. In 1992, Adèle's entrepreneurial world began when she established her own consulting business, working with many of New Zealand's leading corporate and public sector entities and charities by supporting them to create business efficiency and enhanced profitability through people. At its peak, Adèle's company employed 20 team members located between two offices.

2002 saw the arrival of a new phase in Adèle's life – motherhood. That in turn led to the next phase of her entrepreneurial world when she began a 'portfolio career', including undertaking business advisory assignments, coaching small business entrepreneurs, acting as a Non Executive Director for a number of privately owned corporates and charities, and developing a personal property portfolio.

Adèle lives in London with her husband and daughter.

If you would like to communicate with Adèle, please visit her website www.adelemclay.com.

Adèle's social media links are:
FB: Adele M McLay
YT: Adele McLay
LIn: Adele McLay
W: www.adelemclay.com
Tw: @adelemclay

Also From Adèle McLay

Books

Adèle has written other books for **Small Business Huge Success**™:

Brilliant Entrepreneur (Akitu Press)

Personal Brand YOU! (Akitu Press)

Business Tips

Adèle presents free online business tips via her YouTube channel (Adèle McLay) that you are welcome to view. If you would like to receive Adèle's **Weekly Business Tips** by email, please register at www.adelemclay.com

Daily Inspiration

Thousands of people receive a daily inspiration email from Adèle, which hopefully supports and motivates them to achieve all that they dream of — personally and professionally. If you would like to receive Adèle's **Daily Inspirations**, please register at www.adelemclay.com

Interviews of Successful Entrepreneurs

Each month Adèle interviews a successful entrepreneur asking lots of questions about their business success, so that her listeners can learn from the experiences of these successful entrepreneurs from around the world.

If you would like to receive Adèle's **Monthly Interview** Audio, please register at www.adelemclay.com

About Small Business Huge Success™

Small Business Huge Success™ was created by Adèle McLay. Its vision is to provide relevant, accessible and digestible knowledge by way of books, learning programmes, and coaching to business owners around the world who want to learn more in order to achieve the business success and personal freedom they dream of.

As well as publishing a range of books on all topics related to small business success, *Small Business Huge Success*™ publishes home study learning programmes and has a membership site that supports small business owners around the world. For more information, please see:

W: **www.smallbusinesshugesuccess.com**

FB: **Small Business Huge Success**

YT: **Small Business Huge Success**

If you would like more information on *Small Business Huge Success*™, please contact:

Small Business Huge Success™
P O Box 56429
London SE3 9UF
Tel: 0044 (0)203 137 9871
enquiries@smallbusinesshugesuccess.com